Momsie:
The Journey Home

A DEVOTIONAL MEMOIR

Momsie:

The Journey Home

A DEVOTIONAL MEMOIR

Saundra L. Woods

2021

Cover Design: Propel Marketing LLC
Editing: Joanna Sanders LLC
Layout & Formatting: Propel Marketing LLC
Mother's Day Photo 2021: David Trout

978-1-7365094-0-1 (Paperback)
978-1-7365094-1-8 (eBook)

Acknowledgments

I strongly believe that there have been generations before me that prayed for me; for my freedom, my health, my happiness, and my salvation. As surely as I live and breathe, I know my two grandmothers did.

Sincerest appreciation and love to the many sister-friends I have been blessed to share life with. I have a varied cadre of Christian women who have cried with me, prayed with me, encouraged me, and when needed, corrected me. They have stood in place as the sister I never had, the mother I needed, and sometimes, the daughter I never anticipated. They are close and far, frequent and occasional, but always welcome and familiar. Distance and time have no sway on these bonds. I thank ABBA for you, ladies.

I thank all who loved me through these last days with my mom. Especially my husband Kevin, and our sons, Aren and Chayton; three godly men that are following and serving our Lord. I thank our church family, my homeschooling family, my cousins Ronnie and Sylvia, my aunt Sarah, and the One, and only, Jesus Christ . . . my Lord, Savior, Redeemer and my Strength.

Contents

Foreword

In 1951, J.D. Salinger published his iconic novel, Catcher in the Rye. While it happens to be my favorite book of all time, aside from the Bible, the title gives no indication to the depth and significance of the story. Then, somewhere in the middle of the page, about halfway through the novel, you find the gem that explains it all, revealing the heart of the main character in such a stunning way that most readers stumble to find such an unexpected gem. Such has been my experience with Momsie.

As a professional editor and publishing consultant, I am blessed to be in the position where a lot of manuscripts come across my desk. I work with many first-time authors, which also means that I get an array of skill sets and perspectives. Sometimes they are beautifully fresh and simply elegant—which was indeed the case with Saundra's writing.

Yet when the title of Saundra's manuscript came across my desk, Momsie, I was concerned that the childish-sounding title wouldn't reflect a mature work or attract a serious audience. I had some hesitancy about it, but consoled myself by thinking that if there was something to it, that at least we could change the title later.

I now sit in the humbled position to have seen the story explain itself in the beautiful pieces in which God has built it and Saundra has heartfully reflected it. Even though Saundra quickly became a client, I am now the one finding myself asking her for advice for my life more often than not. I've seen her wisdom well beyond the pages; the wisdom of a life lived, lost and found, forgiven and redeemed. Truthfully, I feel like I've barely helped her with her writing. God really has, because I believe He wanted you to be right here, right now, hearing how He can create new out of that which our eyes perceive to be lost, lacking—potentially even gone forever.

I haven't had the privilege to know Saundra for the decades that this story unfolds through. I've only known her as the woman on the other side—truthfully, a woman that in many ways, we all long to be. We all long to be settled, knowing that the end of our stories is so much more beautiful and perfect than what could have been arranged if we had attempted to orchestrate it ourselves. We all long to be able to laugh on the other side. We all long for the closure that Saundra finds with Momsie. Regardless of where you find current stories in your life lacking closure, I invite you to come and see what the Lord has done here. It's beautiful. It will leave you changed, with hope, wonder, and its own gift of a place, where even for a moment, all seems orchestrated and settled with the world.

It has become my honor to be by her side as she publishes this first important novel. But I consider it a much greater honor that she now considers me a friend. I am undeserving of God whispering His hope, love, light, and continued possibilities into my own stories left undone. Enjoy Saundra's presence in this story; her humor, and her gift of a loving heart. My guess is that we're all going to be stunned by the way God brings our stories together, laughing someday with light hearts; finding out that our experience with Momsie was just a small glimpse of His grand plan.

- Joanna Sanders, owner of Colossians46.com, author of *Fire Women*

Introduction

September 2001
Mother-in-law, Willie Mae, and Mom, Louise, with my sons, Aren (8) and Chayton (6)

I observed through two families how life can make you better or bitter. There was a great contrast between my mother-in-law and my mother. Both women had been born and raised in North Carolina. And both, at a young age, had become the heads of their respective households but under different circumstances. Mom felt divorce from my father was her only recourse when I was two. My mother-in-law had been widowed when my husband was only six years old. He was the third oldest of four, the three youngest children were still at home. Naturally, I would not say that my husband's family was better without his dad, but he never heard an unkind word about his father. And although I imagine his mother could have been angry at God, there has never been any evidence of that. My mother, in contrast, was definitely bitter. Perhaps she was angry at what could have been. Maybe she had given my father chances to "fix" things; I don't know. All I know is that the pain and anger ran long and deep in her soul.

The responsibilities of leading a household wore differently on these two women. My mother-in-law had close family ties, lots of aunts and uncles, cousins, close siblings, and in-laws. Mom had her mother and siblings, but none were very participatory. Yet I believe the fundamental difference was that my mother-in-law always had the Lord and her church family.

There was a spiritual disconnect between the generations in my family. Despite both of my grandmothers being believers and active in their churches, neither my mother nor father seemed to have a strong faith in their lives. The faith of the previous generations had no more been passed onto my parents, than I could turn back time.

My mother-in-law was born one year before my mother in a different part of North Carolina. Both had migrated to New York City but my mother-in-law returned to her North Carolina roots after retiring. After 34+ years of marriage to her son, it is safe to say that hers was a loving, faithful, and family-filled childhood. In 2004, my family flew from Pennsylvania to North Carolina on a Saturday in October for her 80th birthday party. The turnout was such a testament to her obvious love and kindness toward many. She was truly a queen for the day!

The Monday after my mother-in-law's 80th birthday celebration, my mother was scheduled to visit her doctor for a pre-op exam. They suspected colon cancer, but Mom was always easily nauseated, and couldn't tolerate the colonoscopy prep for the exam. (For this same reason, we had to have both my mother and mother-in-law babysit together when my husband and I went away for a few days because my mom had trouble changing a loaded diaper without gagging!) I convinced Mom that she shouldn't go to the doctor alone and so early on the morning of November 1, my husband and I drove my van into New York from Pennsylvania. He got out in Manhattan for work, and I continued to Brooklyn to get my mom. Visiting my old neighborhood brought back memories. Some good, some sad.

I had not seen Mom in months, and I was stunned when she opened the door and I saw her skeletal frame. Inwardly, I think I screamed in shock. She had asked that I bring some adult diapers because of her various incontinence issues, but they swallowed her up due to her weight loss.

After getting her to the initial appointment, one look told her doctor that she was a very sick woman. We were immediately sent to the closest hospital, where she was admitted that evening.

Coincidentally, the hospital was the same one I had been taken to at age nine when I had been in a vehicle accident on my way to school. Mom and I recalled the day I went face first into the windshield of my little school van. I had been the only child of the ten or so onboard who was hurt. According to our driver, a car cut him off and he plowed into some parked cars. Stopping abruptly, without seatbelts, I went flying. God was protecting me because amazingly enough, my eyes had not been cut, and although bleeding profusely from my forehead and chin, and the laceration on my neck revealed my pulsating jugular vein, it too remained unscathed. If it had been cut, I certainly would have bled out before anyone could have saved me. I had been knocked out but I quickly regained consciousness and a woman in the crowd took me in a taxi to the hospital. I was alert and able to give pertinent information to the doctors, and they called my mother at her job and waited until she arrived to stitch me back up. I imagine she was anxious as she rode from Manhattan to Brooklyn. I had been able to speak with her on the phone, so maybe that calmed her. She held my hand as the doctor began to suture me up, only admitting later that she couldn't take it, and had a nurse slip her hand in mine so she could compose herself. And here we were, decades later in the same Emergency Room, now me caring for her fragile state.

My husband left work early that day, and met us at the hospital. He and I left Mom there not knowing what was in the future, but trusting God for the road we were all walking.

My mom never saw her apartment again. Never saw her 80th birthday. Never saw her grandchildren again.

My mother-in-law is still with us, as of the time of this publication and only recently stopped driving and just celebrated her 96th birthday!

I have found it is true that God has no "grandchildren." We all must establish our own relationship with Him through our own experiences with Christ; us as children, and Him, as the true Father. While it may be encouraged, or inspired, true faith is not something that can be caught from someone else. You must own it.

What follows are the thoughts and prayers that were revealed to me as I traveled from our home in the Poconos to Brooklyn two-to-four times a week for the last two months of my mom's life and for some time afterward.

This is a story of an unconventional mother-daughter relationship. In spots I have pulled back the curtain and revealed the past so you can see the journey from the beginning and better understand how we found each other in mutual love. I rejoice now in God's perfect plan. To say that He was with me would be an understatement. There were some days when He carried me. Some days He held my hand. Some days He pulled me along. But never did He leave me. There were even days when He told me I could stay home without guilt.

My desire as you read these entries, is that you gain some sense of how even in the blackest of times, God's light is there. Even when you don't want to open your eyes and see the pain that's as solid as a brick wall, He's there for you to fix your gaze upon instead. These divine encounters were not easy to write about. I've attempted to write each in a way so as to not emphasize my story, but rather what He might be doing in yours. I've settled on the term, "passage" instead of "chapter" because truly these were each different journeys within the larger one. My heart is for you to treat each "passage" like a personal devotional. Sit with the short "passage," the scripture that was included, and ponder if God has any message for you in my retelling of the events. Take a day, a week, or whatever time period speaks to you, and with prayer and contemplation, find any nugget of divine wisdom and truth for your own journey.

This life is truly just a vapor.

Child of God - the peace, joy and love of the Lord are always greater than the pain because He is the Great I AM!

In Him,
Saundra

REWIND

When my maternal grandmother was young, her mother died, and her father remarried the proverbial bad step-mother. Living through a difficult childhood, by the time she was eighteen and a man proposed marriage, she jumped at the chance; viewing it as a lifeline. He was an ornery, poorly educated sharecropper from North Carolina. Records vary, but he was anywhere from the same age to twelve years her senior.

My mother was born to them in 1925, the fifth girl in what would be a family of six children. Her only brother was born five years after her.

Family stories would suggest alcoholism and physical abuse in the household. With the youngest girl, my mother, safely sent off to college, Grandma took her son and sought to escape to New York where her other daughters had gone. When my mother found out, she dropped out of college and went to New York. This was 1945 and she was only 20. Grandpa, Pop as we called him, was not to be left, so he followed his wife shortly thereafter.

While tracing my own roots, years later, the only child born on August 13, 1925, my mother's birthday—was a girl named Esther Mae . . . not Louise, as I always knew her. There were foundational disconnects in our relationship from the very beginning and secrets I will never uncover.

In 1948, Mom married my father. Although quite naive, my mother was hired as a New York City Correction Officer in 1957. Their marriage was less than idyllic, and when she got pregnant with their only child (me), in 1958, my father suggested that I be aborted. Obviously, Mom changed her mind, but she was on her way out the door to the "doctor." I was born in February of the next year. By the time I was two, the marriage had ended, and Mom left with me.

Mom and I shared a bed at my maternal grandparents' apartment in Brooklyn from the time I was two until about age seven. "Gamma's" home (as she was called) had been a refuge for many; now it was our turn. She became a staple in my life during those five years.

Momsie modeling her dress uniform

Being a Correction Officer enabled Mom to provide for us without the need of financial help from my father. But I believe that what she saw as a Correction Officer affected her greatly. As a result, I was very sheltered. I didn't attend the local public school or even play with the neighborhood kids. I played by myself. (It is quite difficult to play Trouble or Monopoly by yourself!) I was shipped out to a private school which was miles away each day. Going to school in a plaid uniform and riding in the school van only served to isolate me. The park across the street was forbidden without an adult escort. In her mind the futures of the other girls would be filled with teen pregnancies, drug use and other assorted wayward behavior. Her sheltering didn't actually sway me from that life, however.

After a time, a newly built apartment building opened around the corner, and Mom and I became two of its first tenants. It was a grand building for the neighborhood, complete with underground parking, a laundry room, and a uniformed doorman. It was a jewel in the working-class neighborhood. Mom and I shared a bedroom, as it was cheaper to get a one-bedroom apartment and she said that I didn't need my own bedroom anyway, "since we were both women."

I could actually see Gamma's kitchen window from our second-floor apartment. If I needed to, we could have yelled a conversation to each other across the backyard! It was so characteristic of Brooklyn!

When we were still sharing a bed at Gamma's house, Mom would sneak out on dates. It scared me to wake up alone. I didn't understand why she went to bed with me and then wasn't there. I tried to hold on to the frilly edge of her nightgown so I would feel her leaving. I didn't want to let her go. But of course, I would fall asleep and she would slip out.
As I look at my mother in her hospital bed, I know that I will have to let her go again soon.

Passage 1:
Child to Parent to Parent

My mother, Louise, 79 years old at the time, was admitted to the hospital on the first of November, 2004. As I watched her frail body become diagnosed with one adverse condition after another, I leaned more and more on my heavenly Father. We had not had an idyllic mother-daughter relationship, and we were stepping into uncharted territory together.

A few months prior to my 40th birthday, I accepted Jesus as my Savior. Slowly, the Holy Spirit led me to forgiveness, acceptance, love, and a true desire to share the Gospel with her. September of 2002, my mother accepted Jesus as her Savior, and became a fellow "sister-in-Christ." It was in this place that we finally began to find mutual love and acceptance for one another.

Standing in the same hospital in which she once tended to me, it is only because of the work of Christ in me that I am so differently equipped to handle this. As I listen to the doctors list the myriad of health problems that are certain to be responsible for my mother's demise, I have peace.

At 45 years old, I am both mother and daughter. I have two sons of my own. And I see one more role emerging that I never sought. In God's perfect plan, I can now step with love, reluctantly, but confidently, into the role of being a "parent" to my parent. I see that God prepared me, by settling me in my own role of motherhood to my 9 and 11-year-old sons, in order to equip me to step into this space for her. I pray that for those of you who have or will experience this role change, that you have learned to love as our Father does. In knowing how to love as He does, you can become the loving caretaker your parents will need in their last, and perhaps greatest trial.

I do not know if I could have done what was necessary otherwise. God has matured me and provided me the support that I need. I have a loving, capable, godly husband who I thank God for less often that I should. I have seen him come alongside and cleave to me, as is biblically ordained.

I must step with grace into this new role to which God has called me, and to try to love like He loves.

Listen to your father, who gave you life, and do not despise your mother when she is old.
Proverb 23:22

REWIND

I was led to the Lord by the pastor that had planted the first church I had ever attended. His leading made such a profound impact on me, I could actually begin to see what a father figure was supposed to be. I became a Christian on November 13, 1998 and was baptized the following summer.

Baptism, June 1999, with Pastor Kevin Green

A few years later, I went into my second pastor's office and spoke to him about my relationship with my mother. As a new Christian, I knew I had to address the problems in our relationship. I told him that I knew I should share the Gospel with her, but I honestly didn't want to be the one who helped get her into heaven and I didn't want her in the same part as I was going to be! Truly not a loving or respectful attitude towards one's mother . . . let alone a Christian! Gratefully, with some guidance, I was set on a path to forgiveness and understanding. It also showed me the patience, grace, and mercy that God was extending to me.

My pastor gave me an assignment designed to change my heart attitude towards my mother. The assignment was to complete two lists. The first would contain my expectations of how a good mother would treat a child; and the second would compare how I was treated by my mother. He also instructed me to memorize Jonah 2:8 which reads, "Those who cling to worthless idols forfeit the grace that could be theirs." A more recent translation of the same version states, "Those who cling to worthless idols, turn away from God's love for them." (NIV)

Excerpts of my letter to him follow.

> *Pastor,*
> *I read 1 John 4:7–21. Verses 12, 16 and 20 all point to the inability to hate another yet claim to love God simultaneously. If what I feel is akin to hate for my mother, then I cannot, with the same heart, feel love towards God. I would be a liar. Ephesians 4:17–32 speaks of the behavior of a believer in Christ, especially verse 18 regarding being separated from God because of the hardness of their hearts.*
>
> *It seems to me that there is no gray area when it comes to a Christian's leadings; we must choose. If we are not following God, by default, we are following Satan. One is always prominent in our minds and hearts, so to speak, and therefore if I truly wish to claim the title of Christian—which I do—all non-Christ-like actions must cease immediately. It does not matter what trans-*

> *pired before. It must be buried with the old self . . . without the emotional scorecard weighing all wrongs and rights. Is it safe to say that if an idol is something you hold in higher regard than the Lord, then clinging to my anger causes me to forfeit the grace that could be mine? (Jonah 2:8)*
>
> *My compassion for my mother is increasing. There is a road ahead that makes me uneasy but I realize that's where I need to go...*

This exchange began my road to reconciliation with my mother. Without which, I would not have the memories, sweet and bitter, or the divine encounters I am sharing with you in these pages.

Passage 2:

Why Be Thankful?

My mother was constantly on my mind as we continued to indulge in our Thanksgiving leftovers. It was the day after Thanksgiving. Although food flowed—my sons had uncharacteristically large amounts, even for them, and so did my mother-in-law—there was a string of questions running through my mind about my mother. Does she know it's Thanksgiving? Is she upset that I'm not there? Does she think, like I do, that this is most likely her last Thanksgiving? Or, at best, that Thanksgiving a year ago was the last time she could really participate in the celebration? Whether she did or not, I never knew. Her many system failures were already taking their collective toll and she neither invited, nor wanted to be invited to celebrate Thanksgiving last year.

I remember my first holiday season as a child of God. Almost four decades of hoopla, customs, and meaningless frivolity fell away. Layers of commercialism and sales records and secular niceties showed themselves for what they were; a devilish device to keep our focus diverted from God, His goodness, His mercy, His gift, His Son.

NOT DANCE "AS IF NO ONE IS WATCHING," BUT DANCE AS IF THE GRAND ORCHESTRATOR IS WATCHING BECAUSE HE IS, AND HE LONGS TO DANCE WITH US ALL.

It's not about a parade, a big meal, sports, or shopping lists. It's the daily, moment to moment, critical or superficial, malignant or benign things of life that we must be thankful for. When you truly grasp the meaning of providence—of sovereignty—or mercy, as those pertain to God, you would want to dance every day. Not dance "as if no one is watching," but dance as if the Grand Orchestrator is watching because He is, and He longs to dance with us all.

As I am journeying through this season, I constantly hear my Father speaking to me, giving me insight, giving me comfort, sharing some of His wisdom. One of His messengers said that God being perfect, has no plan B. His way is always the just, best, most opportune way to accomplish His purposes. The most and best for the most. So even though "my way" would have my mother jumping out of bed and returning to her life, that is not the way of our Master for her right now. So, I thank Him for whatever is transpiring with Mom's earth suit because I am assured that her next season will be the most glorious!

Rejoice always, pray continually, give thanks in all circumstances; for this is God's will for you in Christ Jesus.
1 Thessalonians 5:16-18

Passage 3:
WITNESS OF LOVE

THE TWO PICTURES I TOOK OF MY SONS ARE HANGING AT EYE LEVEL IN MOM'S ICU AREA. They are holding a poster board sign that they made themselves, which reads, "Get Well Soon, Grandma! We Love You!"

For grandma's bedside

I am hoping to give her a reason to not give up. I remind her that her only two grandchildren want her to leave New York and come live near us in the scenic Pocono Mountains. Sometimes it works. Sometimes she wants to give up.

I'm the only child of a very ill 79-year-old. I do not have other siblings to help me with this. Yet I have an audience. We are raising our sons with the love of the Lord as a very present fact in their lives. Both our boys accepted Christ as their Savior a few years ago and now at ages 9 and 11 understand—better than some adults I know—the meaning of the Cross. Yet as "wise" as these two are, they are still children and their faith could easily be compromised by either myself or my husband's inability to model Christ to them.

Three or so times a week I venture from our home to the hospital to visit with my mother. It is not easy. I would rather be home and homeschooling them as I have, since they were born. But what would that tell my boys? Honor your parents when it is convenient? Honor them in accord with the palsy-walsy friendship you've had with them all your life? My witness to them now is critical.

And God has brought others to witness. We have had to rely upon our church family for their care, their love, and support as well. My boys have seen the fellowship of believers in action. They have seen our Christian brothers and sisters more loving than some natural born siblings. My mother-in-law has even halted her very full life in North Carolina and ventured more than 500 miles to assist us. As my boys are unknowingly losing one grandma, they are cementing their bond with the other. I see God's hand in this. I am a witness to His goodness, as He continues to bring others to witness in the same way to us.

I'm sure when they get older and look back at this time, it will be a bittersweet memory for them. But I know that living out this perfect plan of God will enrich their lives in ways I cannot yet see.

"The King will reply, 'Truly I tell you, whatever you did for one of the least of these brothers and sisters of mine, you did for me.'"
Matthew 25:40

REWIND

Mom was mildly rebellious. In December 1966, she made news when she attended a formal Shriner's Potentate's Ball at the New York Grand Hilton Ballroom. The reports provided detail of how Mom was escorted into the room in a black satin pants suit with ostrich feather-trimmed bell-bottoms and ostrich feather-trimmed elbow length gloves. Her halter top was complete with a very plunging neckline. I only wish I could fit the suit! As an afterthought, her escort was mentioned in the article as having dressed according to the invitation in tails and a white tie. He was a very nice man; an architect who later got a job in California. Supposedly, he asked Mom to marry him, but she declined.

TUX NO, PANTS YES! — The Shriners evidently succumbed to the charms of Miss Louise [illegible] Formal Potentate's Ball Friday night when she entered the New York Hilton's Grand Ballroom in a black evening pants suit. Ostrich feathers circled the bell-bottomed pants legs and topped the matching gloves. Oh yes, her escort, Eugene Lewis, dressed according to the invitation which required tails and white tie. (Gilbert Photo)

Momsie makes the news

My mother was a beautiful woman and had many suitors after my father. None became a step dad or even a surrogate dad to me. The fear of child molestation kept Mom single and she passed on a few good opportunities to remarry. The distrust that had begun with my father and his unfaithfulness and other behaviors made Mom cautious. Was she resentful towards me? Maybe. Truthfully, she didn't demonstrate any resentment. Or maybe I just couldn't recognize it.

Duty and responsibility to me outweighed her happiness. I wondered if her detachment was nurture or nature? She chose me over the men in her life. But duty isn't always love. At a statuesque 5' 10," Mom was very fashionable. Always in high heels, always well attired. I remember when she purchased a full-length mink coat. It even had her name embroidered on the inside pocket. Thousands! I asked what prompted her to buy it and she replied, "So that when I die, you'd have a mink coat!" I always wondered what the appropriate response would have been to that? "Thanks," or, "When will I get it?" Sadly, I do have it. And although I'm not really a fur person, I would never sell it. It has her name on it in more ways than one. When I do wear it, I wear it proudly, as she would.

Mom envisioned something greater for me than herself. Private schools, Broadway plays, piano and ballet lessons . . . sophistication. When I graduated high school, it was a big deal. The ceremony was held at Carnegie Hall in Manhattan. At the time, the school was one of the most academically prestigious public schools in New York, if not the country. My aunt, my mom, and Mom's long-time boyfriend attended. After the graduation, my best friend's mom invited us to celebrate with them at a local restaurant known for its burgers. Unbeknownst to me, Mom had made reservations at the famous Rainbow Room at the top of Rockefeller Center. We were serenaded by Sy Oliver and his band. The only item I recognized on the menu was chicken—chicken Kiev. I didn't like it, and would have preferred a burger! Not a good finish to the four years of academics.

Now, as a mom, I can totally appreciate the sacrifices Mom made on my behalf. Above and beyond that, I know that my ABBA Father was loving both of us through all of the years that we chose our own paths. He is always with us, whether we acknowledge Him or not.

I never told my mother, but her last boyfriend, Mr. Rainbow Room, was the one boyfriend who actually made advances towards me. He was the longest lasting relationship she had before he broke her heart, and I couldn't bring myself to tell her. It seemed that after all of those years, she had finally let her guard down and opened her heart with him. Nothing ever came of his advances. Once I recognized the snake that he was, I was old enough to avoid being alone with him. I don't think she would have handled it well. She did, after all, have a service revolver and that might have sent her over the edge. I'm grateful for God's hand of protection on us all.

Passage 4: Death and Life, Life and Death

The apple didn't fall far from the tree. Prior to my marriage, and definitely prior to my salvation, I used to say that whatever I wanted to do, I did at least twice. If I didn't like it the first time, I did it again to make sure I didn't like it. Naturally, if I did like something, I continued until I wanted to stop! I will not list my sins, but suffice it to say that I am blessed to be alive.

The Bible tells us of the mystery of free will, selection, election, and predestination. Most of the saved are confused by this divine truth but eternally grateful that they heard and accepted the call to salvation. But what of life and death?

In my self-centered days, I was choosing life in the very temporal sense and death in the very eternal sense. But oh sweet, sweet amazing grace. When I chose to accept a substitutionary death on the cross, I chose life eternal! Hallelujah, hallelujah!

Mom chose the same life—death—death—life path as me. Initially choosing rebellion, we both eventually found our path to life through Christ. What peace I have, that whatever happens, both of us have life eternal in Jesus's presence. Whoever arrives first, will see the other in a blink of their eyes!

"Whoever finds their life will lose it, and whoever loses their life for my sake will find it."
Matthew 10:39

Passage 5:
No Warranty

There are more tubes, wires, cuffs, catheters, tape, and gauze attached to my mother than I would ever want to see. Her sunken cheeks, made more skeletal by the lack of dentures, speak to her frailty. The only contrast is her swollen right arm, the cause of which has yet to be found. Clots in the shoulder area? No one knows. I have lost count of the numerous discoveries that have been made in the last 25 days. If mapped out, it certainly would look like an old computer flow chart. If this, then that. If not, then this, if yes, then that. Each discovery brings about another set of health diagnoses, all bad. Unlike the flow chart that ends in the successful running of a program, hers is more like a 3D cascade failure. Dominoes falling in an uncontrolled, undesirable pattern of chaos.

In Job 14:5 we are assured that our days are known and numbered by God. So, what of illness? How do we view these earth suits?

Clothes serve us in that they keep us decent, hopefully warm, and protected from the elements. They can make us look shabby or make us look good. A used suit that's two sizes too big, out of style, a bit frayed, and dirty will make you decent and warm, but a tailor-made, designer suit will look and wear better. Wouldn't you rather have your own new suit?

Have you attached value to your earth suit? If not, why not? Do you take perverse pleasure in your poor diet and toxic substances? Are you too busy for yourself? Choosing to regulate your health with prescriptions or medicines feigning weakness to control yourself? Do you accept that everything from TVs, to cars, to your body, wears out eventually? The warranty has expired on the TV so that's when it goes blewy! Built-in obsolescence is the cry. But what about us?

If our days are known and numbered then it seems to me that the controllable part of the equation lies in the quality of life. If 79 looks frail and sickly (my mom) but 80 looks vibrant and healthy (my mother-in-law) why? Genes? OK, maybe to some extent, but how can we be used for His kingdom as effectively as possible if we are falling apart? Yes, some things are bound to be subject to age, but wear and tear and the outright abuse we subject ourselves to is within our control.

If your church building is falling apart, what do you do? Do you leave it alone claiming built in obsolescence? Of course not! God's house must be maintained and respected.

Who will stand at the foot of your bed on those last days and what will they see?

WHO WILL STAND AT THE FOOT OF YOUR BED ON THOSE LAST DAYS AND WHAT WILL THEY SEE?

Do you not know that your bodies are temples of the Holy Spirit, who is in you, whom you have received from God? You are not your own; you were bought at a price. Therefore honor God with your bodies.

1 Corinthians 6:19-20

Passage 6:
DIGNITY AND PRIVACY

THE BETRAYAL OF MY FATHER FURTHER REINFORCED MOM'S NEED FOR PROTECTION FROM THE CRUEL WORLD and manifested itself in isolation for her, and over protectiveness towards me. In my experience, I've learned that isolation brings loneliness and overprotection brings mercurial results. And it was true in our relationship. The tighter her grasp, the easier I found a way to slip from it, until, as I said before, I chose my own path of rebellion.

Momsie, age 15

If Mom had had an ideal family life how would that have changed her? I remember her telling me about a very hot August day when she was around eleven or twelve. Everyone was at the local church and the young'uns were on their knees on the wooden floor between the pews. The service was long and it was hot and loud. The "mothers" of the church were all around the children, singing and praising God. The meaning of it all escaped my mom. All she knew was that she felt hot and sick. She said she noticed that every now and then, someone would jump up, hands raised and shouting. The women of the church who were closest gathered them up, fans in hand and took them outside. Not knowing why, she just knew that if she did the same, she would find relief. So, she jumped up! The cool evening air was such a relief! Mom was led to the mill pond, which is exactly what it sounds like. The residual washing from the local mill drained into the small pond, and there she was baptized. But to her, it didn't mean anything. Did it count as salvation? She didn't know what or if anything had happened.

Had she been aware of the saving grace of Jesus Christ in her young life, would she have been so guarded? Would she have questioned God about the pains she experienced? Was she angry? I was angry. I was angry with her for what I felt were injustices in my life caused/created/exasperated by her and what was, in my opinion, her failings as a mother. I felt this way for many years.

But with the eyes of Jesus, I now saw how my life and all of the circumstances that made it mine, were so divinely necessary. If I had not experienced what I did, I would not so joyously treasure and appreciate my salvation. If you grasp that it is all perfect in God's divine plan, you can accept that what you deem as failures on your part, or on the part of others in your life, were part of that perfect plan, and you can be thankful and at peace.

Mom will see Jesus. But lying in the hospital bed with total strangers looking, poking, and prodding is neither dignified nor private. We are not made to be either. The Sadducees and Pharisees were considered "dignified" in their day. They hoarded the Word of God to distinguish themselves and isolated their "knowledge" from others. They created status and idolatry out of positions of power, as though they had some closer access to God. But their prideful actions and treatment of others kept them far from the heart of God. We must remember that Jesus said "the first shall be last" (Matt 20:16). We must humble ourselves as Jesus did—denying His very nature and becoming lowly for us. If anyone should have been dignified, it should have been Jesus. He had no need for it, because He embodied the heart of God.

Although she is no longer independent, Mom is still a strong woman. Now she is strong in the Lord. No longer concerning herself with emotional hurt and protection through privacy. Now she just wants to be with Jesus.

... He will swallow up death forever. The Sovereign LORD will wipe away the tears from all faces; He will remove his people's disgrace from all the earth. The LORD has spoken.
Isaiah 25:8

Passage 7:
Crazy is Relative

I learned the word "eccentric" when I was very young. I think I learned it from a Bugs Bunny cartoon. Elmer J. Fudd had failed for the umpteenth time to catch Bugs Bunny, and eventually he snapped. He thought he was a "wabbit" and was put away to an asylum . . . grey rabbit suit, carrot and all! But because he was Elmer J. Fudd, a millionaire, and owned a mansion and a yacht, he was labeled as "eccentric." I liked that word. Poor people or average people were crazy, looney, or when extremely demented, and incurable—insane. But "eccentric" seemed acceptable.

When a person, especially an elderly person is hospitalized in ICU, they can develop what is called "ICU psychosis." Having been in ICU for a couple of weeks, Mom had it. There were lucid moments. Then "the man with the gun" would show up and she'd "have to move out of the line of fire." The other musings were more bizarre and I need not speak of them.

I have a family member who, as the old folks would say, "had fits." People are generally familiar with the notion of someone "throwing a fit," but that might be comparable at best, to a temper tantrum. These fits though were often violent and threatening. Sometimes glass would be thrown. As a six-year-old witnessing it, it was scary. The only thing that would calm him down was Gamma reading the "red words" from her Bible.

She would face "the fit," as Daniel would face the lions and proclaim the Word of God over it. Like Daniel, she remained unharmed, and like the lions, he would be calm and peaceful. Remembering this tactic, when Mom saw or told me of some unusual occurrence in ICU, I would sing hymns or speak of Jesus over her. She would become calmer and smile.

Whatever insanity of life you are going through—whether you are merely in a valley, or having a fit, or dodging imaginary bullets, or under satanic attack, if you are politely eccentric, or straight-jacketed insane with the trials of your life; if you are punch drunk from exhaustion or tired from erroneously relying on your own strength—be strong in the Lord! If the release of emotion has drained you dry, know this…

Jehovah Rapha, our Healer is there (Exodus 15:26); El Roi, the God who sees (Genesis 16:13); Jehovah Jireh, the Lord, will provide (Genesis 22:14). He is with you; before this, through this, and after this. He is omnipotent—knowing all. Nothing in your heart is hidden from Him and He never tires. Like Elijah asked the prophets of Baal of their god, Is he asleep? Is he busy? Our God is none of those. When you call, He has already answered.

Peace I leave with you; my peace I give you. I do not give to you as the world gives. Do not let your hearts be troubled and do not be afraid.
John 14:27

Passage 8: WHAT TYPE OF BLOOD DO YOU HAVE?

MOM HAD TO HAVE SOME BLOOD TRANSFUSIONS. I found out that we have the same blood type, B-positive. My cousin was at the hospital during one of the transfusions and remarked that most of the family also had B-positive blood.

It is amazing how our Lord created our bodies. Why different blood types? I remember some of my high school and college science curriculum, but not enough to know if there are any special benefits other than universality in donating or receiving, to having a certain blood type.

What type of blood did Jesus have? His blood must have been O; being able to give it freely to us all, the Universal Donor.

And what of us? Some have a fear of this life force; it makes them weak-kneed. The Law spoke of not eating any animal with the blood still in it. But once Jesus fulfilled the law for all, as Christ-followers, we can now gladly spiritually and symbolically bathe in His blood. One power-filled drop would have sufficed, but His blood flowed to cover our sins, the sins of those living on that first Good Friday, and all the sins of all those born since and to come.

Washed in the blood is what we sing.

> What can take away our sins?
> Nothing but the blood of Jesus!
> What can make us whole again?
> Nothing but the blood of Jesus!
> Oh, precious is the flow,
> That makes us white as snow!
> No other fount I know,
> Nothing but the blood of Jesus![1]

We have been magnificently washed in the shed blood of Jesus, and we can sing and rejoice in this day because of it.

Thank you, Jesus, for the red cross of salvation! Are you washed in the blood of the Lamb? Only His blood will cleanse your soul.

Have you fully received your transfusion from the One and only Universal Donor?

In fact, the law requires that nearly everything be cleansed with blood, and without the shedding of blood there is no forgiveness.
Hebrews 9:22

---

[1] "Nothing but the Blood" by Robert Lowry, published 1876

REWIND

If crazy is relative, normal can be also. I don't think it's normal to have seen both my mother and her father so intoxicated that they were crawling through the house on all fours making their way to the bathroom. Pop, my grandfather, would sit outside the building on the garbage cans and drink; often until he wet his pants. I don't know what Gamma said, but on more than one occasion she stood over both her husband and her daughter and admonished them for their behavior. Except for those times, it seemed Gamma was always happy. She read her Bible and was active at her church. Normal. When you are accustomed to dysfunction you learn to "roll with it," you learn that trials, like seasons, come and go. Without the valley there could be no mountain.

Mom smoked and drank regularly. Sharing the bedroom with her meant I didn't go to sleep until her last cigarette was extinguished. With the lights off, I watched as the glow of the cigarette floated from the ashtray to her mouth, brightened with each inhale, and returned to the ashtray. I always made sure it never landed on her bed, or the floor, and that with the last puff, the flame was completely darkened. At one point, with tears streaming down my face, I begged her to stop smoking.

She would try, but it never stuck. Now we both face her untreatable lung cancer. I reflect on my own drinking, smoking, and use of illegal drugs as well, and I thank God that I was able to stop it all. But I can't help but wonder, if Mom had kept her promise, . . . but I can't dwell on that without sadness and regret. The regret of a child whose inability to influence their parent causes them to see the reality of just how important their fears were.

Passage 9: YOU CAN'T JINX GOD'S PLANS

DO NOT BELIEVE IN ACCIDENTS OR COINCIDENCES. In God's perfect plan, He knows all that will happen and what the long-range outcome will be.

Mom is in bed number five. In bed number four, is a woman who like my mom, worked many years for the city of New York. My mom was a Correction Officer; this woman spent thirty years on the police force. Her daughter is balancing the parent-child caretaking role also. And she seems to be at the breaking point. We hold ourselves together emotionally for our loved ones and we want them to hold themselves together physically. We want our moms to yank out the tubes, and rise like Lazarus. Maybe they will.

In the meantime, in our weakest moments, we fear what we dare not think or say. The very thought of being anything but a strong, supportive, advocate shames us. We want the strength of Jesus. But to receive that strength we have to be totally empty. We can't be looking to carry 90% of the burden and ask for 10% of Him. It won't ever suffice. We must be devoid of self. That is not a selfish notion—but a selfless one. We must be at 0% to fully realize His power in us! The enemy would love to have us think that "God helps those who help themselves." This is not Biblical; this is heresy and fallacy. He is not a gap-filler. This faulty notion stands right in the way of us realizing Christ's power to the fullest extent. Less of us is more of Him. It's ok for us to be inadequate because He is more than able.

Still, to say out loud that we've had enough, we almost feel we would "jinx" it—as if God would take commands from us. He already knows what we will not speak. He already knows that we push away that "evil" thought asking to end this. But it is in the speaking and yes, in the whisper or even the silent scream, it is then that we release it, and He can take it from us. To hide those thoughts only exhausts us. It's like trying to hide a beach ball in a tub of water—you tire very easily. All of your energy returns to that unattainable task. God knows those thoughts. The Holy Spirit intercedes for us with groans and utterances that we can't even speak (Romans 8:26). Until you learn that the undesirable, sinful, selfish thoughts are already known to God, and He loves us just the same, you cannot fully focus on His strength in your life. He knows you're angry. He'll help you. He knows your guilt. He brings you peace. He knows you're tired. He gives you rest. The expression: "let go and let God" is true, but you have to

> **THE EXPRESSION: "LET GO AND LET GOD" IS TRUE, BUT YOU HAVE TO LET GO OF YOURSELF, NOT JUST YOUR BURDEN.**

let go of yourself, not just your burden. Let go of it all. Don't worry, He is ready to receive it and He is ready to receive you.

Come to me, all you who are weary and burdened, and I will give you rest. Take my yoke upon you and learn from me, for I am gentle and humble in heart, and you will find rest for your souls. For my yoke is easy, and my burden is light.
Matthew 11:28-30

Passage 10: The Blessings of Abnormality

I believe that my mother's progressively deteriorating condition is a blessing. While surely, it will ultimately lead her into the arms of Jesus, I am determined to see the blessing in this adjustment for the rest of my family here. I believe it is serving us well to have been taken out of our routine, at least temporarily.

Very few of us truly enjoy prolonged chaos. Sure, every now and again a little spontaneity is great, but there is comfort in routine. Humans are creatures of habit. A lot of us have a hard time parking in a different location at our local supermarket, changing our seat at church, or being forced to take a detour to our regular destinations.

Caring for Mom at the end of her life has imposed a massive interruption to our routine. And my husband, like many men, wanted stability for our family. I love this about him. I love this man that God sent me. Through his headship over our household, we have both learned many things about what a Biblical marriage looks like.

The role of spiritual head of our home was always important to my husband. When we married, although I wasn't saved at the time, we made a serious commitment. I knew the verse from Genesis about leaving your father and mother and cleaving to each other. But only due to the ongoing process of Christian growth and discipleship, did I begin to understand and truly live by it. My husband is not always vocal about our love, nor is he directly demonstrative, much to my dismay. I have to glean from his routine actions how he feels. I've had to learn how I am to respond to him, he to me, and us both to Christ. Early on in this trial, when our routine became interrupted, I felt I was battling my husband and I was beginning to resent it. I wondered why he couldn't see my perspective on the adjustments that I believed needed to be made—including an abbreviated school day for my sons. We weren't on the same page initially; yet after years of marriage, I knew we had Someone to intercede for our unity.

So instead of talking to my husband first, I went to the Father. I did not pray for my husband to be changed. I asked that any wrong on my part be revealed to me. And then I left it at the foot of the throne.

The very next day my beloved spoke to me. God had revealed to him that he was trying to make everything normal. He could no more make this abnormal situation normal, than he could hide that aforementioned beach ball in a tub of water. He was frustrating himself and me.

In the routine of life, do not become too comfortable. Comfort breeds complacency. And complacency leads you to forget to fully rely on God. I'm sure Noah, his wife, sons, and daughters-in-laws could have thought of another way to spend a hundred years rather than to put their lives on hold and build an ark! I'm sure one of them at some point cried out for normalcy to return. But Noah was following God's plan.

Try as he did, my husband could not make our life normal again. Not even part of it. He would have to gather us into our ark, and ride out the storm. Our lives would forever be changed, but they were changed according to God's perfect plan.

Now listen, you who say, "Today or tomorrow we will go to this or that city, spend a year there, carry on business and make money." Why, you do not even know what will happen tomorrow. What is your life? You are a mist that appears for a little while and then vanishes.
James 4:13-14

REWIND

I grew up in the days of the phonograph. No CDs or DVDs, not even many cassette players. I treasured the old vinyl LP's Mom played. Her collection was vast and probably contained some rare or semi-rare recordings. Usually on Saturdays when we cleaned the apartment you could hear the music in the hallway. Sometimes in the evenings when she fixed herself a drink she would dance around the room. I could name tunes that my peers had never heard of.

Out on the town

Probably the reason we wound up at the Rainbow Room listening to Sy Oliver and "his band of renown" was because Mom loved jazz. I imagine she fancied herself as one of the grand dames of Harlem in its heyday, heralded by the music of Duke Ellington and Count Basie. In fact, my paternal grandparents' house was not too far from Count Basie's in Queens, and they had a mutual connection with him. The family lore was that as a toddler, I sat on Count Basie's lap at his piano.

Of course, I don't remember this, nor is there photographic evidence of it. Nevertheless, I would often brag to my classmates that I sat on his lap.

Growing up, there were only six clear channels on our television, so we would often listen to one of Mom's comedy albums for entertainment. Bill Cosby was one of our favorites because of his wholesome comedy. We listened to his records so frequently, I was able to repeat the routines myself. I still remember most of them.

In one of his albums that we enjoyed frequently, he recounted the births of his two daughters. Their first-born girl, Erika, was such a joy that he told his wife they needed to hurry up and have another one. And then he explained:

> *"Now this second one, Beelzebub. First of all, she come out of the chute a month early, champagne in one hand, a cigarette in the other."*
>
> *"Awww right! Who's in charge here? You, the ugly guy, what are you doing here?"*
>
> *"I'm your father."*
>
> *"Get rid of him Momsie!"*[2]

That line and his description of her behavior that followed always had us in tears of laughter! And from that point on, my mother, who had actually gotten rid of my father by leaving him, was "Momsie!"

---

[2] Bill Cosby: Revenge, Warner Bros. Records, Inc., a subsidiary and licensee of Warner Bros. Pictures, Inc., 4000 Warner Boulevard, Burbank, CA; 321 W. 44th Street New York, New York 1967

Passage 11: MOMSIE

FROM ABOUT AGE TEN, I BEGAN TO DISTANCE MYSELF FROM MY MOTHER. I believe this was the result of being teased by an older cousin about being my mother's baby. In retrospect, I realize these taunts came from someone who had been disowned by their own mom and probably was jealous over my relationship with my mother. I think those taunts had such an impact because I valued that person's opinion of me. More than 15 years my senior, we shared the same home when I lived with Gamma and was basically my primary playmate.

As adolescence crept in, it was quite easy to expand upon the rift and distance between myself and my mom. When I moved out for the last time on my 20th birthday, I severed all ties from my mother for about a year. I'm certainly not proud of the years that followed, but I understand them now, and if given the choice, I actually wouldn't change them, because I understand God's sovereignty. When I resumed communication with my mom, it became easier to flippantly refer to her as "Momsie."

My use of the name "Momsie" acknowledged a role, but not a real respect or affection. After we reconciled, and we were both Christians, I continued to call her Momsie, but I noticed I said it differently, with love. One day as she lay in her bed in ICU, she began to cry. She wanted out of the hospital, out of the sickness, out of the pain. She just wanted out. It broke my heart. I said, "Don't cry Mommy." I had returned to the preten-year-old title of "Mommy" which I hadn't said in its true context in 35 years.

Mommy.

The event brought to mind an incident I witnessed many years ago in a deli. A man in his twenties was arguing with his girlfriend. The police somehow got involved, and while handcuffing the struggling man in front of the store, the man's forehead broke the plate glass window, and he began to bleed heavily. From inside the store, I heard his voice change from blustering vibrato to childlike desperation as he cried out, "Mommy, Mommy. Help me Mommy!" I never forgot that.

I wasn't a mom at the time, but even now years later as I recall this scene, I cry a mother's tears that always wants to help, no matter how old the child has grown. The bond between parent and child can be so strong, yet so fragile. Each has the power to exalt or deflate the other. Now having come full circle with my own mom, I realize there were times we each wanted to save the other. But there is salvation in only one name. And there is one parent-child relationship that never waivers, is not fragile, and never can be destroyed. He's calling you. His tears and His blood were already shed for you because of His love. Will you answer? He's listening and it is not too late to cry out "ABBA, Father, help me!"

Out of the depths I cry to you, LORD; Lord hear my voice. Let your ears be attentive to my cry for mercy.
Psalm 130:1-2

Passage 12:
Clearance

THE LORD IS OUTSIDE OF TIME. Can you understand that? He sees the beginning, the middle and the end of everything simultaneously. Only He knows what will be in eternity. And He knows it all, right now! Awesome. Trying to see "the big picture" is as close as we can get to being outside of time. Clearing out my mom's apartment was an unexpected "big picture" view of some of her life, in hindsight.

As I consider the changes made to my mother's apartment through 37 years, I flash through mental images and memories like a scene from the 1960 movie, H.G. Wells' The Time Machine. Things moving quickly, some appearing, and others disappearing. Night, day, night, day, summer, fall, winter, spring, night, day, night, day. And then it stops. Regardless of how this hospitalization ends, I have to face the apartment I lived in for twelve years as a girl, and clean it out.

A preliminary look into her closets tells me the things she

held onto have value only to her. The things I thought she would have kept, are gone. We can clutter up our homes, and cars, and lives in total with such meaningless "stuff." All the things that keep our eyes off Jesus. The amount of money thrown away on items that only have sentimental value to their owner is astronomical. We cling to status and ownership as though they were sources for internal worth.

Why do we find comfort in stuff? Why do we find status in stuff? Why do we measure wealth in stuff? Can you say you have total comfort and joy in Jesus? Can you accept and behave as an heir to the Kingdom of God and live accordingly? Do you know how wealthy you are as a co-heir of God's Kingdom? What price would you pay for all the riches of the world times a million? Well friend, it's already paid for, and it's yours for acceptance. When all the stuff is cleared and you can see the "bigger picture," like I believe Mom does now from her hospital bed, will you thank Jesus for paying the ultimate price of separation from the Father for your sake, for the sake of your inheritance?

"Do not store up for yourselves treasures on earth, where moths and vermin destroy, and where thieves break in and steal. But store up for yourselves treasures in heaven, where moths and vermin do not destroy, and where thieves do not break in and steal. For where your treasure is, there your heart will be also."
Matthew 6:19-21

Passage 13: Get the Lead Out!

As a birthday prize at Sunday school, I ordered some novelty pencils to give to the students. These pencils had an eraser at both ends and written across the sides were the words, "life, like this pencil has no point without Jesus." It clearly illustrates the first part of a Christian walk; acceptance of Jesus and the invitation for Him to come into your life. A godly woman at my church took the illustration further. "Like this pencil," she said, "you must be broken, to be used in God's hand." How true!

Many of us accept salvation and think we've checked some sort of spiritual box in life, and the work is done. But God tells us that's only the beginning. We have lessons to learn, messages to share. Like the pencil, we will need to be sharpened to be used well. I heard someone say you have to "have a mess to have a message." We have to be broken, humbled before we can acknowledge our need for God. Then we have to be put through the grinder where all the useless dead wood is rubbed and scraped off to expose the finest, sharpest point. Then we can write the message with our lives that God has us here for.

Yet, the truth is that some of us prefer to stay in the pencil box. It's safe. We won't get broken or sharpened. We won't get used to a nub. But those pencils leave no mark on the world. "Well done my good and faithful servant" (Matt 25:21) doesn't apply to them.

But those who get out of the box, and lay in the Father's hand, those are the ones He'll lovingly break, carefully sharpen, and joyously use.

For we are God's handiwork, created in Christ Jesus to do good works, which God prepared in advance for us to do.
Ephesians 2:10

Passage 14: Don't Doubt the Divine

DO YOU DOUBT THE DIVINE? One cold evening at the hospital I was particularly ready to go home. Mom was sleeping, or at least trying to, and had been uncommunicative for hours. As I made one last trip to the hospital lavatory, I started talking to the adult child of another ICU patient. Sensing that this was no quick conversation, I reconciled to the fact that I'd be getting home even later than anticipated. I had a three-hour commute and the next bus would leave an hour after the one I was shooting for. But I knew for certain that God wanted me to continue the conversation. In our small group study, we are encouraged to see where God wants us to join Him in His work. As our conversation continued, I knew that I was divinely in the right spot. My prayer is that I got out of the way and that my responses were all from the Holy Spirit, not me. I found myself hugging a complete stranger and praying in her ear as we quietly wept.

To experience God in such a manner is humbling. To honor God should be our utmost desire. The Scripture says, "But first and most importantly seek (aim at, strive after) His kingdom and His righteousness [His way of doing and being right—the attitude and character of God], and all these things will be given to you also" (Matt 6:33 AMP). When you honor God with your obedience, He will honor you.

Incredibly, I still made my bus. God knew all along. But we must not doubt the divine. There was a play out years ago entitled, "Your Arm's Too Short to Box with God." I never saw it, and I really don't know what its message was about. But the title holds true. Why do we fight the God of the universe? Why do we think like Sarai, that we could have a better plan and better timing than God? Why do we try to ease His burden? How outrageously arrogant we can be! Humility is realizing that we need God and knowing that without Him in everything, we are lost. Not just "lost" as in confused, but truly lost to the fiery pit of hell, in eternity. Without Him, there is no hope.

Appreciate the power of the cross, the meaning to God of His Son's death and the inexplicable, inexhaustible love of God for us.

In a large house there are articles not only of gold and silver, but also of wood and clay; some are for special purposes and some for common use. Those who cleanse themselves from the latter will be instruments for special purposes, made holy, useful to the Master and prepared to do any good work.
2 Timothy 2:20-21

REWIND

Although beginning my life living with my paternal grandparents and remaining close to them after the divorce, they never mentioned their son. I never asked about my father, and Mom had started off telling me he was dead. The truth slowly came out, and when I was ten, I met him after his mother died. I was coming down the stairs in my Nanna's house when in walked a man. Mom did the honors. "Harvey, this is your daughter Saundra. Saundra, this is your father Harvey." We shook hands. Not exactly how one should meet their father.

Girls need their fathers for a reason. A loving, hopefully godly father will help her establish her self-worth. He represents God as one who loves unconditionally and does battle for his little girl. Without that influence, girls often grow up as I did; insecure in their value and abilities, and unconvinced that they are loved. Unprepared for life.

As a child, I had a natural tendency towards meekness. I was not an advocate for myself and generally did not perceive my self-worth as significant. I did not feel like there was much room for discussion when difficulties would arise between my mom and I, so, to deal with my frustration, I did two things. Sometimes I would kick her bed, as if it were her. The second thing was "riskier" in my childish mind. We had a large three-foot-tall lamp with an equally tall, black shade in our living room. I lightly wrote a few curse words on the inside of the shade. Whenever I felt angry, I would look at the shade and believe that I was "cursing" at my mother. I'm not sure that either "hell" or "poop" would have caused torrential discipline if they had been discovered, but they gave me some satisfaction nonetheless.

Pet cat, Tabby, and the Cursing Lamp

Passage 15: Boot Camp

I HAVE NEVER BEEN IN THE MILITARY. But like many other civilians, I've seen the movies and shows that expose the rigorous training new inductees go through in Boot Camp.

Why such harsh, mind and body numbing verbal and physical humiliation? Why do these young men and women have to be treated in such a manner? Because their minds must be conditioned to follow commanders. They must learn humility, to not think of themselves first, but of the whole objective and of their comrades, to rely on and help one another. They must make certain physical sacrifices that will get their bodies to respond automatically to stresses and strains. The disciplines of proper diet and exercise and rest must be strongly cultivated. They must be prepared for war.

About three years ago, one of my sisters-in-Christ and I noticed profound changes in each other. Our spiritual muscles were strengthening. Our minds were transforming to the mind of Jesus. It seemed like we were in a spiritual boot camp. A necessary preparation for war. Would we be called up? We almost feared what would lay ahead for us as if we were being prepared for combat. If she had not gone through boot camp willingly, as I did, she would have lost the battle when she found out that her child had been sexually molested by a trusted neighbor. And I would be losing this battle to stay strong for my mom and my family during Mom's illness.

The disciplines of daily feasting on the Word, prayer, resting in Him, fellowshipping with other believers, and even service are all endeavors that keep us prepared for our battles. As soldiers of the cross, we have a responsibility. Are we going through boot camp half-heartedly? Are we skipping some of the exercises divinely designed to strengthen us? And if you're in the battle right now, are you listening totally to your Commander, the Holy Spirit? Or are you drawing up a "better" route around the gunfire? He sees the entire battlefield and He knows the enemy's plan of attack. Relish every moment of your boot camp training and learn to rely fully upon and obey your Commander.

Finally, be strong in the Lord and in his mighty power. Put on the full armor of God, so that you can take your stand against the devil's schemes. For our struggle is not against flesh and blood, but against the rulers, against the authorities, against the powers of this dark world and against the spiritual forces of evil in the heavenly realms. Therefore put on the full armor of God, so that when the day of evil comes, you may be able to stand your ground, and after you have done everything, to stand.
Ephesians 6:10-13

Passage 16: **No Apologies**

We had a testimony time at church this past Sunday. I wanted to express to the congregation how much God has done in my life during this trial, but I never want to appear arrogant. Before I could speak, my husband did, and I was grateful for that. His words spoke of the visible strength I have gotten from the Holy Spirit during this time. He said it in such an eloquent and humble way that I was able to receive his praise for the blessing that it was—a reflection of God's good work in me. My desire is always to reflect Jesus to those around me. Would Jesus deny that He was the Son of God? Would He boast that He was the Son of God? He stated fact—so must we. If Jesus is Lord of your life, live as if it is so. If the Holy Spirit is clearly working in your life, let it be known. If you thank God, the Most High for everything, then take no credit for yourselves, but give God the glory.

I feel compassion for my brothers and sisters in Christ who feel the proper posture is to not speak of the joy and strength they have in Christ Jesus during their most difficult times.

Are you ashamed that God is working in your life? His love is being manifested in and through you. How is your light to be seen as a reflection of His, if you do not credit the source? Do not hide your blessings for fear of human jealousy or criticism. We are to follow Paul when he said in Galatians 6:14, "But God forbid that I should boast except in the cross of our Lord Jesus Christ" (NIV).

I have not crumbled because I spent years loving my mom less than I should or honoring her less. I have not crumbled, only because God loves me, and honors me, and I, Him. God has restored the years the locusts have eaten.

We do not need to make apology for the work He's done in us, or the blessed robes we get to wear because He is clothing us in His holiness. We need only to boast in the cross.

"Therefore everyone who hears these words of mine and puts them into practice is like a wise man who built his house on the rock. The rain came down, the streams rose, and the winds blew and beat against that house; yet it did not fall, because it had its foundation on the rock. But everyone who hears these words of mine and does not put them into practice is like a foolish man who built his house on sand. The rain came down, the streams rose, and the winds blew and beat against that house, and it fell with a great crash."
Matthew 7:24-27

Passage 17: **Ghetto**

I DIDN'T KNOW I HAD GROWN UP IN A GHETTO. People often associate the term "ghetto" with poverty, crime, and hopelessness. However, I learned that a ghetto is any area where the inhabitants are of the same ethnic or economic group; hence the Warsaw ghetto during the Nazi reign. The Brooklyn neighborhood of my youth had working class people, and brownstones, and responsible homeowners. They took pride in their surroundings, in their appearances, their decorum, and often in their faith. Sure, there were a few who abused the system, and abused various legal and illegal substances, but primarily, it was a safe, clean, and encouraging neighborhood in the sixties. By the time I left at age 20 in 1979, the decay had begun. Little by little, the pride and care of the neighborhood diminished; and now as I visit Mom's apartment of 37 years, I disassociate myself from what I see.

I've lived in the mountains of Pennsylvania for 14 years and for the last 12, have not ventured back into New York City except to resign from my job and to see an off-Broadway show. When I take a breath, I'm now used to clean, crisp air. I know the smell of soil. I know the contentment of hearing my own pulse mingled with a gentle breeze. But back in my old neighborhood, I smell the things I recognize as poison to my mother; fried fish, fast food, cigarette smoke, spilled liquor, and garbage. I look on the ground and see not grass, and ants, and acorns, but canine feces, discarded food, and cockroaches. I ache that in this chapter of Mom's life, these are the things that assaulted her senses. Although I would love to go back in time to when she could have moved from this place, or change the current circumstances so that we could move her now, I do not hope for either.

As much of a contrast as my country living is to her city dwelling, I still know that my country living is rubbish compared to the mansion awaiting me with our King. I truly rejoice that Mom has a place prepared for her too, and that she will be welcomed with open, eager arms. What sweet smells and heavenly sounds await her for all eternity! I can only endure her leaving, knowing that her next stop is Heaven, and I will meet with her in the sweet by and by. Will you be there too? Your loved ones? Love is an action verb. Take action. No matter where we all came from or end up on this earth, God loves us and sent His Son to bear the full weight of all of our sins. Let your loved ones know that.

"Do not let your hearts be troubled. You believe in God; believe also in me. My Father's house has many rooms; if that were not so, would I have told you that I am going there to prepare a place for you? And if I go and prepare a place for you, I will come back and take you to be with me that you also may be where I am."
John 14:1-3

REWIND

Mom was never demonstrative with affection. Her currency of love was just that; currency, money, things. I remember at age nine or so asking her why she didn't cuddle and soothe like mothers on TV shows did. She actually asked me to demonstrate as if it was a foreign concept to her. That was a very uncomfortable scene. Preteen me trying to show my own mother how to mother. I never asked again. I inwardly felt that if I pushed, the truth that she didn't love me would come out.

One evening while riding in a friend's car, we saw a dog that had been struck by a car on the highway. In its shock, it just stood frozen in the road and we narrowly missed it. Sitting in the back seat, all I could envision afterwards was the poor dog; scared, hurt and more than likely receiving no aid. No mercy. No love.

I began to cry. I was a "silent" crier. Only children such as myself, are often trained to be seen and not heard. Unless you were paying attention, I wouldn't be noticed. After getting home, Mom finally saw the tears and asked why I was crying. The question came from a distance, as Mom sat on her twin bed across from mine. I just cried.

Inside, I desperately wanted her to not ask because she should know her own child's sensibilities! I just wanted her to hug me, rock me, tell me it was ok. I wanted her to save me, as I would have wanted to do for that dog on the road.

Neither of us received comfort that night. The dog probably died that night . . . part of me did too, I think.

Passage 18:
Tears from Heaven

It's a wet, rainy day as I travel in to see mom. On December 1st, most people are planning their Christmas shopping and decorating, and party planning. While I do consider the shopping to be done for my kids, my primary focus is on the days ahead as they pertain to Mom. Will this dreary day be the day we tell her she has untreatable lung cancer? Will the tears flow like the rain? This afternoon, the sun is supposed to return, along with high winds. If this morning is filled with tears, this afternoon will be filled with the Son and the Holy Spirit.

My tears will be for what will not be. She will not see 2005. She will not be here much longer. When my father died in 1999, I was the only relative to be found to sign his death certificate. I cried then. Not necessarily for his absence as much as the lost opportunity to have a father on earth. At least my mother and I can say that we were a family.

Who cried when Jesus was beaten, whipped, spit upon, and nailed to the cross? I am assured that all tears will be wiped away and that Mom will be received into God's presence because of the sacrifice that had been made for her two millennia ago. I already know that the tears I will shed at her funeral will be more of joy for her than of sorrow for me.

The Bible says, "Do not be ignorant when those fall asleep" (1 Thess 4:13), and "Rejoice, for when the saints are absent in the body, they are present with our Lord" (2 Cor 5:8). No matter what has happened in our earthly experience, the tears of Heaven will be tears of rejoicing.

Night Momsie became a Christian - Sept. 27, 2002
Women of Faith Conference, Philadephia, PA

"'He will wipe every tear from their eyes. There will be no more death' or mourning or crying or pain, for the old order of things has passed away."
Revelation 21:4

Passage 19: THIS PATH

As a Sunday School teacher, Proverbs 3:5-6 was one of the first verses I learned alongside my students: "Trust in the Lord with all your heart, and do not depend on your own understanding. In all your ways acknowledge Him, and He will make your paths straight." (ISV)

God gave me a personal insight into that verse long before my mother's hospitalization. New believers can often mistakenly feel that all should be fine and dandy once they accept Christ. More experienced believers know that concept is both untrue and unbiblical. The Bible confirms there will be testing, refining, and loving discipline from the Lord all along the path. There will be teasing, ridicule, isolation, and sometimes hate and jealousy even from friends and family. I tell my students that a path can have divots, potholes, obstacles, dark spots, highs and lows, and still be straight. God doesn't say smooth and flat. Our straight path is the path to Him; in us not turning to the left or to the right. No detours. Detours present themselves when we cease to trust Him with all our hearts; when we start to try to figure it all out, and when we stop finding God in the mundane. As the verse says, He makes our paths straight. It's His direction, not our own, that keeps us on the straight path.

I know I am walking the path God has laid out for me because I know that this is God's perfect will. I know that He is in front, beside, and behind me all the way. I know that if I tire, He carries me. I know that if the storm begins to rage even more furiously, that He will calm me, if not, the storm. And I know, truly know, that this path leads me straight to His heart. What a perfect destination. What a perfect path, no matter what may come.

By faith Abraham, when called to go to a place he would later receive as his inheritance, obeyed and went, even though he did not know where he was going.
Hebrews 11:8

Passage 20:
JUNK MAIL

I PICK UP MOM'S MAIL EVERY FEW DAYS. Credit cards offer 0% interest! Sale on now! Save 20%! Come to the casino—get a free night's stay! Look your best with Glamour Wigs!

I smile at the frivolity of it all. Don't they know that in the large scheme of things, what they peddle means nothing? My mother is dying. I know they don't know that, but when you look at all of the earthly focus our energies are expended on, it should make us take a step back. If every true believer pooled their resources, swallowed their pride and publicized Jesus and the cross, where would the world be? Billions are spent on advertising things that leave us broke, empty, and envious. In contrast, salvation restores, fills, and brings us peace. Like the loaves and fishes, the more we share the Gospel, the more we receive from the Gospel. Why do we hide our Master's light behind our shadow of propriety?

Mahatma Gandhi, a devout Hindu, once said: "You Christians

have in your keeping a document with enough dynamite to explode civilization, to turn society upside-down, to bring peace to the war-torn world. But you read it as if it were just good literature, and nothing else."

God's letter to us is not junk mail!

I would rather live in a way that advertises my next life than my "prosperity" in this one. If someone calls me a "Jesus freak" I will gladly thank them. At least then I know that what I believe is visible. May your neon sign forever proclaim and publicize Jesus, Jesus, JESUS!

This is what the LORD says: "Let not the wise boast of their wisdom or the strong boast of their strength or the rich boast of their riches, but let the one who boasts boast about this: that they have the understanding to know me, that I am the LORD, who exercises kindness, justice and righteousness on earth, for in these I delight," declares the LORD.
Jeremiah 9:23-24

Passage 21:
Eyes of Jesus

I have learned some valuable lessons to not lean on my own understanding, or even the thoughts of others. Similar to the prompting of the popular acronym WWJD, (What Would Jesus Do), I have learned to step back and assess situations, trying to look as Jesus would first look at them.

Like a lot of families on earth, mine is dysfunctional, and has a long history of it. Having lived with Gamma from age 2 to 7 and then just around the corner after that, I clearly remember the family tradition of Sunday afternoon dinner where we would all come together to enjoy her cooking. Almost every Sunday dinner was a family event. Usually my aunts, uncles, and my three cousins came by and it was delightful. One of Gamma's best dinners was the fried chicken she prepared before church. I could barely wait until she got home so we could eat.

Then she died. And I remember as early as her funeral, seeing odd behavior from her children. There was anger and resentment and things I did not understand, even at age seventeen. Recently, a cousin told me that Gamma had predicted this behavior. Sadly, she knew the pretense of unity would end when she died.

When you are only exposed to another person's view of life, such as a parent's view, you tend to adopt that view, especially if you trust them. When you stretch your adult legs and are more exposed to other's lives, you realize everyone's views of life are colored from their unique perspective.

Certain assessments of one aunt in particular had become fact in my mind based on the limited view I was exposed to. However, because of my mother's hospitalization, I have been blessed to see my aunt through my own perspective, not family folklore. I am now trying to look through Jesus's eyes at her and I see that the view is different. What I see is a woman who, through trials and tribulations, has a love for the Lord, and a demonstrative faith. God carried her through divorce, remarriage, two mastectomies, widowhood, and other earthly trials.

Whose eyes do you look through? Our sin-colored eyes are not worthy of the Christian moniker. When we crucify ourselves so that Jesus may live in us, we must take His whole anatomy. We must see with Jesus's eyes, listen with Jesus's ears, touch with Jesus's hands, speak with Jesus's lips, and love with Jesus's heart. Then, and only then can we ask, what would He do?

And he died for all, that those who live should no longer live for themselves but for him who died for them and was raised again. So from now on we regard no one from a worldly point of view. Though we once regarded Christ in this way, we do so no longer. Therefore, if anyone is in Christ, the new creation has come: The old has gone, the new is here!

2 Corinthians 5:15-17

REWIND

At age thirteen, when Mom found out that I had lost my innocence, I imagine it was a betrayal of sorts. To this day, I can see the disdain on her face. It still hurts if I linger too long.

From that age on I received my affection from males. Always taller than my peers and looking and acting older than I was, I caught the eye of many. The male partners didn't ask my age. Why would they? Plausible deniability. "She looked eighteen!" or "I didn't know!" would have been a believable defense. Although I don't know if Mom knew or simply guessed that I was sexually active, she never confronted me about it after the first encounter. The trust had been broken anyway.

By the time Gamma was widowed, she had moved from the old apartment building to a brownstone owned by one of my aunts. Still within walking distance from our apartment, I loved spending time with Gamma. I even stayed with her when I had my tonsils removed and my mom had to work.

Beloved grandmas
Gamma and me / Gamma and Nanna on my birthday

At age sixteen, a junior in high school, I had the dreamboat, jock boyfriend. He was co-captain of the basketball team, 6'7" full of muscle and ego. I believed we would be together forever.

Mom hated him. Quickly he became "Lurch," the stoic butler from the Addams Family. Truthfully, he never tried to ingratiate himself with my mom. I later found out that Mom's instincts were justified; there was great dysfunction in his family. Emotional and physical abuse were in my future. But that's for another time.

In the summer of 1975, my mother got my Gamma involved in my love life! I don't know what she told her specifically, but I had to sit with my beloved Gamma and hear her words of disappointment. I could not tell you what she said. I just saw the look on her face; a similar look as my mother had, three years earlier. I burned with anger that my Gamma knew that I had become disobedient and disrespectful to my mom.

My frequent habit of visiting Gamma stopped after we had had our talk. I was embarrassed and ashamed. In the fall, I found myself pregnant. One morning when I was throwing up in the kitchen sink, I desperately wanted my mother to ask why, to probe, to maybe even guess, and tell me it was going to be alright. When she questioned me, I simply said, "I think I have the flu," and she accepted that. My heart sank.

To me and the NBA hopeful, the only course of action was to abort. And I did so, of course, without Mom's knowledge. Roe v Wade had just passed a few years earlier and it was the easy way out. We had accepted the marketing. It was not a baby. It was only something to be removed so you could go on with your life. No harm, no foul. Years later, God showed me just how wrong I was.

In the spring of 1976, after avoiding Gamma for months, I was driving with my mother and as we passed a few blocks from Gamma's house I fought, what I now believe, was the Holy Spirit's urging to ask Mom to stop by Gamma's home. I remained silent. Gamma died that night.

I blamed my mother for the lost opportunities to spend time with Gamma. And especially robbing me of the last chance I had to see her alive!

I graduated high school in June of 1976 and attended college in the fall. Unfocused in school, and having turned 18 that February, after two semesters I decided college was not for me. As so many prodigal children do, I took my meager savings, and declared my independence. A few months later, having fallen flat on my face in the failure of job loss, and facing eviction, my mother rescued me and brought me home. Of course, I resented that. A year-and-a-half later, on the morning of my 20th birthday, I moved out and vowed never to HAVE to live with her again! I even listed a few unsavory things I would do before I would settle for that fate once more! With that declaration, I left, and I didn't speak to her for a year.

Time softened my hard heart and I finally reached out to Mom and we began communicating again. But our relationship had suffered the strains of rebellion and dissatisfaction and regret. Although we spoke more regularly, there was not a strong, loving bond.

Other sexual partners came and went for me. There were other terminated pregnancies, and Mom never found out about her lost grandchildren. I was still searching for unconditional love.

Passage 22:
Rock-a-Bye-Baby

We all know the song:

> Rock a bye baby
> On the tree top, when the wind blows
> The cradle will rock!
> When the bough breaks, the cradle will fall,
> And down will come baby, cradle and all!

What a lovely song to sing to your child!

Consider this—our lofty, haughty images of ourselves place us high in the treetops. We like the view. The inaccessibility. The "Yertle the Turtle" effect (see Dr. Seuss if you don't know King Yertle!) The trials of life will indeed toss us back and forth. Sometimes very gently and we get an adrenaline rush from the anxiety. But then the Nor'easter comes and what we have built up—our bough—cannot hold us and boom! We come crashing down. The song doesn't give us a happy ending. Like

Humpty Dumpty, we often lay broken, and unfixable, and forgotten rotting on the pavement.

Sometimes He's there to pick you up, and sometimes He has to let the shattered pieces cease their random movement before He gathers them and lovingly glues you back together with the super glue of the Holy Spirit.

But, did you ever wonder, in this nursery rhyme, where are the baby's parents? Well, when you accept Jesus and are adopted into God's family, God's huge hand is there for you, even if your earthly parents are absent (or absent-minded). Sometimes He steadies the cradle. Sometimes He catches you. Sometimes He's there to pick you up, and sometimes He has to let the shattered pieces cease their random movement before He gathers them and lovingly glues you back together with the super glue of the Holy Spirit. Whatever the degree of interaction, you are touched by Father God. You should not remain unchanged. All that transpires in your life is known by Him who is eternal, and outside of time. And all will be used for His glory. God never removes Himself from you, and whether still in the tree, or scattered and broken on the ground He sees you, He loves you, and will never leave you. Psalm 27:10 tells us that even if my father and mother abandon me, the LORD will hold me close.

For I am convinced that neither death nor life, neither angels nor demons, neither the present nor the future, nor any powers, neither height nor depth, nor anything else in all creation, will be able to separate us from the love of God that is in Christ Jesus our Lord.
Romans 8:38-39

Passage 23:
MARTYR'S ROBES
ONE SIZE FITS ALL!

HAVE YOU EVER HAD THE INTESTINAL FORTITUDE TO SINCERELY ASK GOD TO SHOW YOU YOUR SIN? When faced with a relationship problem, do you typically ask God to "fix" the other person? In this season of trials with Mom's illness, I was tempted to do just that. The Holy Spirit convicted me to pray not for my husband and his stubbornness, and not for my mother and her seemingly uncaring nature, but for myself, and my sin-surrounded heart. Certain in my salvation, I didn't believe that sin could entirely push Jesus out of my heart, but I knew it certainly could encamp around the compound and clog up the lines of communication!

What was revealed to me, was my sin in the form of my pious attitude; my false martyrdom. The things I was doing for my family and my mom, I did sacrificially. It was my duty. The evil one can make the duty of a Christian their trap. Oh, woe is me; look at what I have been called to do without self-regard. Ain't I special? How had I slipped into that quagmire? Easily. I looked away from Jesus. I was too busy looking in the mirror. And when I did, I saw a lonely wife with no energy for her husband. I saw a church worker, who was constantly reminded how difficult things were but that I was "strong" and God would see me through. I saw a daughter who jumped into the parental role for her dying mom without segue, in what felt like too much too soon. What I did not see, was Jesus. Somewhere along the way, He had been passed by and was no longer leading. My burden became my idol.

SOMEWHERE ALONG THE WAY, HE HAD BEEN PASSED BY AND WAS NO LONGER LEADING.

Oh, what shame and disgust I felt at that revelation. But what grace God had shown! I recognized how much He loves me to show me my sin. Knowing that His love was still as strong as ever, I knew I was forgiven! What blessed assurance.

What burden has become your idol? What act of perseverance has come between you and your Lord? Remember, we are to crucify ourselves daily—moment to moment. Then, and only then, can we keep Jesus at the center of our life.

Therefore, my dear friends, flee from idolatry.
1 Corinthians 10:14

Passage 24: ROACHES RIDE THE SUBWAY

I HAD JUST TAKEN MY SEAT IN A SEMI-FILLED SUBWAY CAR AND AS I LOOKED AROUND, I NOTICED a small object rolling around in the seat opposite me. The two passengers on either side of the otherwise vacant seat seemed oblivious to this movement; I don't know why. Maybe that's part of the don't-look-around-mode New York riders get into. Me? I constantly scan. Well, the "rolling object" was actually a bug. To be exact, a North American cockroach. As I watched the roach walk to the edge, disappear under the seat, and reappear, another passenger sat down in the unoccupied seat. Not knowing exactly where this bug had gone, I couldn't shout a warning, so I just watched.

Sin is like that bug. Even a small roach on someone psychologically causes you to think that person is unclean. It didn't have to come from their home. They could just innocently have brushed up against where the bug was. We must be vigilant in our casual, day-to-day lives. There are bugs everywhere.

There is a popular movie and the family name used in the title sounds close to a four-letter word that is quickly becoming part of casual speech in the secular world. Whenever the name is said on TV, our minds are automatically drawn to the other word. Coincidence? Humor? Subtle sin. If you have such things in your memory, they surface. When they surface, they compete for space with the things Paul told us to think about—things that are noble, praiseworthy, true (Philippians 4:8).

Sin can be subtle like a little bug that attaches itself to you, unaware. It can be seen by others, and will cause them to view you not as a representative of Jesus, but as just another reflection of the world. Be vigilant in your walk that the bugs that seem harmless don't creep in and stay.

> **SIN CAN BE SUBTLE LIKE A LITTLE BUG THAT ATTACHES ITSELF TO YOU, UNAWARE.**

Blessed is the one who does not walk in step with the wicked or stand in the way that sinners take or sit in the company of mockers, but whose delight is in the law of the LORD, and who meditates on his law, day and night.

Psalm 1:1-2

REWIND

In 1985, by divine intervention, I met a godly man and we got married in 1986. I wanted my mother to give me away. She had done everything she could to fill the void of my father, and the honor was due her. However, after years of not knowing where my paternal grandfather was, we found him just before the wedding, and Mom insisted that he give me away.

June 28, 1986

A few years later when my husband, mother, and I were visiting Grandpa in the hospital, my father walked in the room. I tell you the truth, the room got colder—even my husband felt it. The look on my mother's face was the same look I saw from her when I was thirteen years old. She was still very bitter after almost 40 years.

My husband and I moved to Northeast Pennsylvania in 1990. Our first son was born in 1993 and I became a stay-at-home mom. Holding him for the first time flipped a switch that opened the floodgates of love that only a parent, a mother, could understand. And with that, I began having nightmares.

I would often wake up crying or in a rage. Why? In my dreams I would see my mother walking up our driveway. I would begin cursing at her, refuse her entrance, and slam the door in her face. How could a mother hold their child and not love them? How could a mother not want to cuddle and soothe their baby? Becoming a mother only made me wonder why it had been so difficult for my mother to show me love.

It angered me that friends who had babies had their grand-mother, mother, sister, aunt; someone to help them. When I shared my experience, friends would look sadly at me with incredulity sprinkled with pity. I spent the first months of our son's life figuring out what to do with a newborn by my-self, but I loved everything about it! Our son was about six months old when my mother met her first grandchild. We drove into NYC and visited my mother-in-law, and Mom met us there. Even with him, she was visibly detached. Her touch actually made me cringe and recoil. I had no faith in the sincerity of her affection. Our second son was born in 1995, and again, Mom met him months after his birth. Never had she asked to come visit, never had she invited us to come see her. Never did she ask if she could help physically. She sent clothes and checks, but not herself. The tragedy was that Mom didn't get to see how special motherhood could be.

The ways of mothering and childbirth had changed signifi-cantly from my birth, to my sons' birth. Mom told me that she had been knocked out completely and when they woke her to present me to her, she reached for me but her arms were strapped to the table and she couldn't hold me. Although natural, breastfeeding was discouraged, so she never did.

It was quite the opposite with my deliveries. It has caused me to wonder about the psychology and physiology of maternal bonding.

Ironically, Mom and I became mothers at the same age in our lives. Vowing that I would not be an older mom as she was, I still wound up repeating the same pattern. When I was born in February 1959, my mother was 33, and turned 34 that August. My first son was born exactly one month before my 34th birthday. I remember envying a high school classmate whose mother, grandmother and great-grandmother, were all 16 years apart. She rejoiced when she turned 17, and hadn't had any children, breaking the family cycle.

I used to think I shouldn't be a mother because I often spanked my dolls. Yes, I was spanked as a child, sometimes with a belt, but I was never a victim of abuse. It didn't happen very often, but that was the way of the sixties. The "switch" (a cleaned thin branch from a nearby tree applied forcefully to the seat of one's pants) was the preferred method of discipline in the south among the previous generations in my family. My maternal grandma's experience with her stepmother may have begun the tradition. Curbing the instinct to hit as a means of discipline was not easy, but I did, and the tradition ended with me. I'm grateful that we have one standard of perfect parenting, in our Heavenly Father.

Passage 25:
STEP SKIPPING

THIS TRIAL WITH MY MOTHER'S ILLNESS BEGAN ON MONDAY, NOVEMBER 1. Eight days before Christmas, on a sunny Friday evening, she was able for the first time, to get out of bed, and sit in a chair. That following Monday morning, she lapsed into a coma and was not expected to recover. I had prepared myself, through God's provision, for her passing weeks before she was even diagnosed with lung cancer. But I realized I skipped a step or two.

Man's way is often described as a five-step process for grief. The true name was "The 5 Stages of Receiving Catastrophic News," as penned by Elisabeth Kübler-Ross in her book, On Death and Dying[3]. They are: denial, anger, bargaining, depression and acceptance. Others have scripted similar patterns, sometimes including choices regarding how to carry on without your loved one.

---

[3] Kübler-Ross, Elisabeth. *On Death and Dying*. United Kingdom: Scribner, 2011

As a Christian, I started at "Stage 5" acceptance. I wasn't in denial; I didn't get angry. There were no bargaining sessions with God and I may have been sad, but I didn't get depressed. I could see a sense of disbelief in the doctor's eyes as he told me Mom's many issues and the prognosis, and I seemed to be taking it "so well." Convinced that I understood his words, he looked at me, questioning. His yarmulke told me that he knew of God, so I shared my faith with him. He nodded as a rabbinical student would and smiled.

I know God is sovereign. I know God doesn't make mistakes. I know that God's plans are perfect, I know God has me in mind and that He loves me. And I believe that God will be glorified more if I live what I profess to believe and go straight to step 5!

I am no super Christian. A friend once called me her "spiritual hero." They saw me as a hero because they wrongly assumed that I had gone through the steps instead of bypassing them with faith. I deny that title. I turn and run from that title. A hero does the extraordinary under their own power. I do not claim that ability. If I appear strong, it is my faith in God that this streams from. It is only by faith can I empty myself for Him. If I am crucified to self, and allow Christ to totally fill me, I am not a hindrance to His work on this earth. It is only by His strength and love can I go straight to acceptance. It is only in the full knowledge of my surrender could I walk this path. It is not I, but Christ in me.

I have been crucified with Christ and I no longer live, but Christ lives in me. The life I now live in the body, I live by faith in the Son of God, who loved me and gave Himself for me.
Galatians 2:20

Passage 26: Without Variation

GOD MADE ALL OF US SO MUCH ALIKE AND YET SO DIFFERENT. Most of us have eyes, ears, a mouth, hair, teeth, two legs, and two arms. And yet the most subtle variation changes the way someone looks, or how attractive they may be considered.

Momsie is now a shell of her former self. In her heyday she turned heads, stopped traffic, and could easily be described as "sassy." She was tough, stern, and very likeable. For a formal affair, she didn't buy "off the rack." Instead, her black satin pants suit had been commissioned for her . . . ostrich feather-ringed pants and feather-trimmed, bicep-high gloves and all. Who does that? But now. Oh, what variation, even in our appearance throughout our life. Variation can be unsettling.

Before salvation, I stayed on the science side of life. Mathematics was always my favorite subject. If A+B=C, it always did. No discussion, no opinion, no sometimes; just a set, constant formula that always worked. Religion was too dependent on "ifs." That is still true. Christianity is very different though; it is simple. That's the beauty of God.

We have sinned. God is holy. Sin cannot commune with holiness. God is just. Punishment must be meted out. Perfect Jesus, as God incarnate, came to take that punishment for us all. It is the gift He gives us. When we recognize that we cannot be "good enough" and accept the free gift of salvation, God allows communion with Him while in the flesh, and forever more in eternity.

Without Jesus, we are condemned. With Jesus, we are forgiven. We all will live forever. Where, is up to us.

Beauty is often said to be in the eye of the beholder. What about faith? When the storms of life come—and they always will—what do others behold when they see you? Is the joy of God reflected in your darkest storm? Joy is not dependent on circumstances. Joy is a state that can be arrived at, through faith and understanding of who God is. You can be sad and have joy and peace. Sometimes, I may appear detached, or analytical, or cold. But I have plugged into the formula. There is one answer, no matter how many variables there are. The answer is Jesus. Run through the equation and you always come up with Jesus. No one else can cleanse me. No one else can pay my debt, no one else can bring me peace. No one else can be the sustainer of my joy. No one else. Just my Jesus.

THERE IS ONE ANSWER, NO MATTER HOW MANY VARIABLES THERE ARE.

Jesus answered, "I am the way and the truth and the life. No one comes to the Father except through Me."
John 14:6

REWIND

My mother was the type of mom who could look at you from across the room and you would freeze in your tracks! I proudly inherited that ability as a mom, and could halt my boys from a distance of 30 feet! But she had another quality; fearlessness. Or at least the look of fearlessness.

Momsie about age 21

In our neighborhood there were some "colorful" characters. One such character would sometimes attempt to attack a New York City bus as it passed our building . . . often wielding a knife. The bus drivers must have known about our neighborhood assailant, and would just continue to inch up on him. I was often afraid when we were out and he appeared; never quite knowing when he might decide to attack. But Mom didn't flinch. When I asked her why, she said "He's not that crazy! When the bus starts moving towards him, he eventually goes back to the sidewalk!" I figured that Mom could identify "crazy" and so I would be alright.

Years later I found myself relying on her fearlessness. Funny, although I would have denied having a loving relationship, I still felt she was the one person I could rely on in a pinch.

Poor judgment had me in a "fatal attraction" scenario with a 6'9" lothario and I had a very unwelcome guest move into my apartment. The only recourse I had was to ask, plead and beg my mom to come over, gun on hip, and make it clear that he was unwanted.

That day she was my own one-woman cavalry and I was thankful for her.

In my mind I still didn't see it as love, but duty.

Passage 27:
Defining Tragic

JUST AFTER CHRISTMAS, A STAR ATHLETE SUDDENLY DIED AT THE AGE OF 43. I understand the shock of the unexpected. But I continually heard the word "tragic" in relation to his death. According to Webster's, tragic means: deplorable, lamentable—like a tragic mistake, a disastrous conclusion that elicits pity or terror.

What bothered me most about this, was that this man had been a very vocal minister. He had established himself as a God-fearing man. I didn't know him personally, and I never followed his football career. And although only God knows our hearts, I believed what this man professed to be true in his life.

Anyone close to me, knows who I am in Christ. If they were close enough during this time with my mother, they also know my reliance and security in God's sovereignty.

For a God-loving, Holy Spirit-filled human to go home to be

with the Lord is a joyous event! It cannot be viewed any other way by someone who understands the ways of God. No terror or pity, no mistake, not deplorable.

The morning of September 11, 2001, my husband was heading for the Twin Towers. As I watched them fall on TV, I had a decision to make. Was I watching myself become a widow? What of our sons? And God showed me I had a choice. Faith or fear. The two could not coexist for a child of God. Which one would win? I chose faith. Today, if my husband suddenly dies, the word "tragic" will not come from my lips. I would wonder why, and would wonder how I was to proceed. But I will not consider a tragedy having taken place.

When my mother's spirit leaves her body there will be rejoicing. Not only for the cessation of suffering, but for the fulfillment of joy. The promise of God will be what I will be thinking of! Will I cry? Yes. Will I miss her? Oh, yes! But the comfort God gives me outweighs any human selfish sorrow. Why would I choose the struggle of corporeal life when there is the ease of heaven awaiting?

Mom will not live to see her 80th birthday in August, or my 46th in February. She won't see her grandsons turn twelve and ten in January, and September, respectively. She will not be present in two years when I plan to renew my wedding vows for our 20th anniversary. And she won't know that 2004 has ended and 2005 has begun.

She will know the glory of God! And she will be in heaven forever.

No longer will there be any curse. The throne of God and of the Lamb will be in the city, and his servants will serve him. They will see his face, and his name will be on their foreheads. There will be no more night. They will not need the light of a lamp or the light of the sun, for the Lord God will give them light. And they will reign for ever and ever.

Revelation 22:3-5

Passage 28:
THE GREATEST PARTY

AFTER ATTENDING CHURCH FOR A FEW MONTHS, I SPOKE TO MY PASTOR CONCERNING CHRISTIANITY. I phrased it like this: "I know there's a party going on, and I know I'm invited, but I don't know how to get in." On November 13, 1998, I found the "Way" in and officially joined that party. Ever since then, I have considered being a Christian as being part of the best party ever! The guest list is staggering. The VIP list has only one requirement—belief. There are no bouncers, the joy never runs out, and peace is available for all. But as fantastic as the party is, there's still another room. An upper room, located in heaven, if you will. If the earthbound church is having a party, the eternal after-party in the upper room is better still! The only requirement is to wear your very best glory outfit—leaving the constraints of flesh behind.

On December 30, 2004 at 11:55PM, my mom moved to the upper room. I imagine her immediately dancing among the angels. Humbled by the glory of God, did she stare, mouth agape? Or did she raise her arms in triumphant victory over death? Did her ears ring as the angels called to her? Did she recognize Noah, Abraham, John, Peter, or Paul?

Has she searched the cosmos as we know it in the blink of an eye? Or did she even care to gaze upon anything other than Jesus? Is she smiling at me now as I wipe away my tears? Does she know I am so very happy for her?

New York City and the world are all abuzz with the approaching countdown to 2005. As millions prepare to celebrate another chance to diet, another chance to break old habits; my family and I have begun our celebration a day early. When I received the call from the doctor telling me Mom had passed, a tear rolled down my face. I turned to my husband and simply said, "Mom is home."

When the perishable has been clothed with the imperishable, and the mortal with immortality, then the saying that is written will come true: "Death has been swallowed up in victory."
"Where, O death, is your victory? Where, O death, is your sting?"
1 Corinthians 15:54-55

Passage 29: VIEW-MASTER

I REMEMBER MY VIEW-MASTER. If you've never had one, it was a marvel of stereoscopic 3-D technology at the time! Looking similar to the virtual reality goggles of today, you would hold up the View-Master to your eyes, as you would with binoculars. You inserted a cardboard "reel" with seven pairs of small transparent color photographs. Viewing each pair simultaneously created a colorful 3-D picture. I stared endlessly at the demo disk that came with it. The images were so realistic. After examining every millimeter of each scene, I would turn the disk around and examine the reversed image. The loud click of the lever emulated a camera click as I "took my 3D pictures." Sometimes I would try to slowly change the image as silently as possible without the loud click. Never could.

In the View-Master of my mind, I have the 3D images of the last times I saw my mother. I "click" from the lively goodbye, and multiple kisses, to the frozen image of a comatose woman. The reflexive cough, and the subsequent open eyes alternate on my mental View-Master. Both bodily functions give rise to hope; they are only echoes of life. I wish I did not have those comatose images to recall . . . but I do.

The blessing in those is the stark contrast. In a sense, they are the mirror images of each other. One lively, alert, reactive. The other, frozen in existence—merely present in body. Second Corinthians 5:8 tells us that to be absent from the body, is to be present with the Lord. There was such a contrast that it seemed to provide an understanding of the separation of body and spirit. I believe that before her body ceased functioning, she was already more with God, than with us here. We must embrace the truth of our creation. The flesh is constructed from dirt, but without the breath of life—the spirit, God's impartation of Himself, we are truly nothing.

Then the LORD God formed a man from the dust of the ground and breathed into his nostrils the breath of life, and the man became a living being.
Genesis 2:7

REWIND

Despite the rough times with Mom, I do have happy, and even silly memories. I can recall almost wetting myself as I watched Mom intently and deliberately scooping the overflowing water from the toilet back into the bowl! She began to admonish me for laughing, until she realized the futility of her actions! As odd as it seems, now when I have a clogged toilet, I am quick to smile because of this hilarious memory.

When I was growing up thermometers were made of mercury filled glass tubes. You either placed them under the tongue or for the most accurate reading, rectally. The most practical way to sterilize them was to wipe them with rubbing alcohol. Mom, not to be lax in her care for me decided to go one step further when I was sick one time. She placed the thermometer into a pot of boiling water! If you don't get the visual, let me help. The mercury rapidly expanded past the highest possible human temperature mark and exploded out the top of the thermometer breaking the glass and leaving bubbling mercury dancing on the water! We had a good laugh. Fortunately, we also had another thermometer!

Hot water, trouble, can destroy some things. But I've learned that God uses trials to perfect us.

Living in Brooklyn, public transportation was more convenient than having a car, but late in life Mom did get her license and a used 1972 Buick LaSabre. She never could parallel park that battleship and would wait for a local young man to come out and park it for her. When she did get a parking spot in our building's underground parking, there was a solid concrete pillar on the driver's side that she had to maneuver around. It was with fear that she regularly backed into that spot. Of course, one day the pillar got the better of her. As she turned the wheel, she scraped the pillar. Not to panic. For about 10 minutes she went forward and in reverse until there was a sizable, pillar shaped dent in the rear passenger door. She eventually had to get a neighbor to help her park. Years later, when she sold me the car for one dollar, it was still there; a badge of honor and a humorous reminder of my mom.

Classic Rust - $1

Passage 30: WALKING DART BOARD

DID YOU EVER HAVE A DAY WHERE IT SEEMED LIKE EVERYTHING WAS GOING WRONG? Or at least not as expected? Those are the fiery darts that come at us. It usually doesn't come like a cannon blast that takes you out in one fell swoop—but instead as little sharpened darts of the evil one designed to wear away at your armor, point by point. That strategy of his can be very effective. Just as small, constant drips can create a hollow in the hardest stone; our faith can be worn away if we are not vigilant.

During the course of closing out my mother's estate, I made countless trips to her apartment. The six-hour round trip commute soon lost its novelty, and I found myself sometimes sleeping more on the bus, than in my own bed at home. It was particularly challenging when I had to be in Brooklyn by 8 AM one day to await the pickup of the bulk of Mom's belongings by a Christian organization. I was given the time slot of anywhere between 8:00am and 4:00pm, so I had to be there early.

This meant traveling by 3:30 AM, rousing my two sons, and delivering them, bleary-eyed, to my friend's home by 4:00am. The 5:05 bus pulled out on time and made a record setting trek to New York. Suffice it to say, I got very little sleep that morning, because before I knew it, we had traversed New Jersey! Although I was indeed grateful to not be late, I was exhausted having not slept more than 45 minutes. Dart 1.

I had arranged with the superintendent of Mom's building to take certain pieces of furniture—including the dining room set, complete with hutch and server. Because I was doing my best to separate what was being donated and picked up that day from the rest, I used the table to hold items and had left the glassware in the china cabinet. To my surprise upon arrival the superintendent said he didn't want the set. I needed to clean it out for the pending pickup—which could be any moment! Dart 2.

The super sent his son with a hand truck to retrieve the items I was giving him. Culturally we differ. To him it seemed quite appropriate for this young man to "shop" in my mother's apartment. "What's this?" "May I see that?" "Are you taking this?" "May I have that?" I wanted to yell, "Stop touching her stuff!" I didn't. But it still felt very uncomfortable. Dart 3.

3:45PM. No truck. I called and was put on hold until 4:25, at which time I hung up. I called again and got the recording telling me their business hours were only until 4, and to please "call back another time." Dart 4.

I packed my belongings and headed to the bus station. Just making the 7PM bus, I inched my way to the back, to an aisle seat. I try to get the aisle seat because I have knees that give me trouble. I also have disc problems with my back. At 5'10" it felt to me that these buses were manufactured in Munchkinland, and my knees were painfully pressing on the back of the seat ahead of me. Politely, I asked its occupant to give an inch—which he did, literally, but I was still very cramped. After bending, lifting, and kneeling all day, I was in pain and it was going to be a very long ride home. Dart 5.

The driver had the heat on . . . very high. Dry roasting high. I'm dying. Dart 6.

I only had two hours of sleep; and although in pain, and hungry, and beginning to melt, I craved sleep above all else. But two rows back on my right, was a commuter who talked loudly the entire trip. I glanced back to see if he was talking on his cell phone, because I heard no one else in the conversation. He was not. He was talking to the person next to him. Why he had to speak so loudly, and the other person did not, I can't imagine. Ear plugs and pulling my hat down upon my head only served to make me hotter, nothing more. Dart 7.

As I hobbled off the bus, pain radiating from my back down into my hip and knees, I looked forward to listening to some music in my car, but I could not get the CD player to work. I tried in vain for fifteen minutes. Nothing worked, and the Christian radio station didn't come in where I was. Pulling out of the parking lot, I drove in silence until I was closer to home and could get a clear signal. Dart 8.

When I arrived home, I was met with various articles of children's clothing strewn onto the back of the sofa—speckled with paper mache paste. I guess they hadn't seen the old shirts I had packed for them that morning to protect their clothing. And the paper-wrapped balloons were apparently still wet when their gloved hands picked them up, and cradled them against their good coats to come home. Dart 9.

I knew I had to make a choice before I blew my top. So that day, I acknowledged the friendship that allowed my boys to be in a caring home as I traveled. I acknowledged the efficiency of the driver whose God-given talents got us to NY safely, and early, so I wouldn't need to rush. I acknowledged that I had accomplished cleaning out the china cabinet and now needed only to box up the glassware and dishes. I acknowledged although the people I encountered were different than I, that I could choose to put aside cultural differences, see beyond exteriors, and show Christ's love in all matters. I acknowledged that "our stuff" is just that—stuff. Not precious when looked at by the Light of the World. I acknowledged that I got a lot done that would not have been done, had moving men been present, and now I am able to donate more. I acknowledged that the super was able to take other items his family needed, and my friend who had come the day before was able to return, and pick up the remainder of what I had given her. I acknowledged that some trials I must just endure, and any pain, discomfort or "thorns in my side" are nothing compared to the agony of the cross that I avoided because of God's love for me. I acknowledged that prayer and praise works because as I felt my flesh's desire to scream out, I chose to let my soul cry out to God, who answered and renewed my peace. Mile by mile, decibel by decibel, degree by degree. I acknowledged that God knows what is best in all things, and that sometimes we need silence to prepare our hearts, for a radio message or a favorite song of praise and relaxation. All in His time. I acknowledged the witness my attitude created as I joyfully endured, even when I felt otherwise.

Our Christian walk consists of steps and choices. At each step, we can choose to follow Christ. We can choose to acknowledge

God's sovereignty. We can choose to allow God to be right. (He is anyway!) This day, I chose Christ. Was it easy? No. But I can do all things through Christ who strengthens me (Phil 4:13). The "all" includes every mundane, annoying, nerve-rattling task that we need to go through with grace, humility, and joy.

Each of us must choose Christ. Not once, but moment to moment. In doing so, those fiery darts are extinguished one at a time. Our enemy doesn't always use big things, but just enough little ones, like the proverbial last straw on the camel's back, to break us. Enough little things can defeat you or can produce enduring trust, lasting faith, and a testimony to God. Your choice.

Dear friends, do not be surprised at the fiery ordeal that has come on you to test you, as though something strange were happening to you.
1 Peter 4:12

In addition to all this, take up the shield of faith, with which you can extinguish all the flaming arrows of the evil one.
Ephesians 6:16

Passage 31: What Difference Does It Make?

As I went through my mom's things, I was constantly finding old lottery tickets and records of winning numbers. I knew she played the lottery a lot, I just didn't know how much. There had to have been a small fortune in losing tickets there. How many had she thrown away? I once heard that if you did win and you could prove how much you spent on losing tickets, the losers would offset your winnings. For example, if you won one million dollars but had losing tickets that totaled $999,999 you only paid taxes on the $1. Don't know if it's true or not, but it's the sort of thing that would cause my mother to keep so many old tickets.

I stopped playing the lottery before I was saved because I was tired of losing. When I played, I claimed that I was "contributing to the senior citizens of Pennsylvania" (as they advertise it), but I was really just hoping for material riches. I tired of the frustration of playing and missing by one number, or forgetting, or not being able to play and "my number came out." I can't tell you how many times "my number came out" and I hadn't played!

I noticed that Mom's birthday, 8-1-3, once "came out." And I wondered, what difference would it have made? We've all heard the sad tales of rags to riches to naked! How many wished they never would have won? If Mom had won, would she not have gotten sick? If Mom had won, would it have been easier to clean out a mansion than her apartment? If Mom had won, would she have felt the need for a Savior?

If Mom had won, would she be in heaven?

It is often said that God has three answers for our prayers: yes, no, and wait. I don't know if His answer to her was "no," or "wait," but I do know Mom didn't win the lottery. Instead, she won the victory!

IF MOM HAD WON, WOULD SHE BE IN HEAVEN?

Store up your treasures in heaven, where rust and moths and thieves cannot go (Matt 6:20). I know that that is where I will find my riches!

"For I know the plans I have for you," declares the LORD, "plans to prosper you and not to harm you, plans to give you hope and a future."
Jeremiah 29:11

Passage 32:
DIVINE CONNECTION

WHEN GOD'S HAND IS ON YOU, YOU CAN'T ALWAYS TELL UNTIL HE REMOVES IT! Leaving Mom's one night, my husband and I loaded up the rental truck and started on our four-stop journey home. At the first stop, we donated bags and boxes of clothes, household items, and the like, to a charitable organization. Having not stopped for lunch, we were quite hungry by 5:30pm and picked up some fast food from across the street. Although wanting to sit at a fine establishment, we prepared our meal in the cab of the truck, and attempted to start off. To our surprise, nothing happened. We had a dead battery. While we waited for the company to send assistance, we ate together in stillness in the middle of a busy street in Brooklyn! Help finally came, and by the time we got started, the sun was caressing the horizon, and we just wanted the 100+ miles to be a memory.

We quickly found out, though, that the electrical system in the truck was failing. Our headlights were growing dimmer and dimmer, as the night got darker and darker. By the time we were half way home, we were a hazard to ourselves and anyone else on the highway. We were alerted by the honking of horns as others would come upon our darkened truck and had to pass us. And then, it started to snow.

We found a 24-hour gas station—with no working public telephones and using our cell phone, called the rental company again with our newest location and situation. (Good thing we're still not waiting there for them!)

As we sat with the engine running—we dared not shut it off—we prayed. Our cell phone batteries were about to die out, it was 9:00 at night, we were cold with only a minimal amount of heat, and we were 75 miles from home in the snow. What else could we do but pray?

I've found that there are prayers that resound in my soul like a low chord on a pipe organ. It is as if I can feel the Holy Spirit echoing my prayers in God's throne room. It is those prayers when I can "feel" the answer come upon me like a gently-placed gift. These are the prayers of surrender. The prayer that has no limit; no codicil; no compromise; no bargain. These are the prayers of the humble, the meek, the sinner. These prayers simply let God know, that you finally know, in every cell of your being, that He, and only He, matters. That He, and only He, is your hope, your refuge, and your salvation. These sweet-smelling prayers get answered with a "WOW!"

My husband went under the hood and within five minutes, touched a wire and the lights blazed! Excitedly, I yelled through chattering teeth, "What did you do?! What did you do? Do it again!" With that, the lights stayed lit! He got in and we drove home.

It was not his hand, but God's, that restored the power. Like that engine, we need to be connected to the Power, to the glory of God, forever. We are but dim hazards to ourselves and those around us without that Divine connection. Our lights must not grow dim in this darkened world. We must stand and shine wherever we go, whenever we go, for as long as we go!

WE ARE BUT DIM HAZARDS TO OURSELVES AND THOSE AROUND US WITHOUT THAT DIVINE CONNECTION.

"I am the vine; you are the branches. If you remain in me and I in you, you will bear much fruit; apart from me you can do nothing."
John 15:5

Passage 33: Close the Door

SOMETIMES LIFE FEELS LIKE A SERIES OF EVENTS, SECTIONS, CHAPTERS, AND SOMETIMES ROOMS TO BE CLOSED OFF. People are quick to tell us, "Move on. It's in the past. Can't change it. Forget it." How can you do that? The Bible tells us God forgives and remembers no more. He's God. We're not.

In the months following my mother's death, my life marched on, but my mind kept going back. I kept reaching back, holding onto fading memories. I don't like change. And a lot more than my mother not physically being in my life had changed at the same time. I had to clean out 37 years of memories from the only place we called "ours." She loved her 1975 Cadillac—gone. I said goodbye to the neighborhood that held the only childhood memories I had; knowing I probably would never return. And our family church was changing as well. While our church building project had brought forth a magnificent structure for God's Kingdom, the little cramped storefront church that I was saved in, was also gone. My children were saved in it as well, and it was the only "church home" we ever knew. Even though it was "new and improved," it was still very different to me. And to be honest, I hated it initially. The congregation had gone from about 60 or 70 when I first came, to almost 200 and growing each week. New faces. New personalities. I felt lost... and unloved.

The more change was upon me, the more I wanted to cling to the past. And the more I looked around, the more reason I could see to do that. A car passed with personalized plates, "LOUISE," Mom's name. A movie was released which, of all things, focused on the Women's House of Detention in Greenwich Village. The first job Mom had as a Correction Officer, was at that women's prison. Were these taunts or loving memorial stones placed by God?

I tried to close the door to the past, only to find it was a revolving door. And with each turn, it scraped at the wound, opening it once again.

I got tired. I got tired of being a Christian. Now that's not something I'm proud of, but it happened. I knew firsthand that life with Jesus was infinitely easier than life without Him. He had sustained me through the roughest part of my mother's illness and her death. But to allow Him to do that kind of work in your life requires something. Having an intimate relationship with Jesus is no different than with a friend or spouse. It takes time, effort, communication. And I no longer wanted to do what it took to maintain the close relationship. I didn't want to pray or read the Bible. I didn't want to go to church. I just wanted to be left alone. Have you ever felt that way?

The door (to our past) should be made of glass. We have the ability to remember, and to learn from the past. We are not meant to go back and live there, but we are not meant to forget entirely either.

What I found was that God keeps His promises. He knew how I'd feel. He knew what it would take for me to look fully upon Him again. And He knew I'd fight it. I wanted to pout and be left alone. He would not forsake the one, not even for the ninety-nine; and He did not forsake me. I could walk my own path finally, with Him, and be at peace with departing from the past.

HE WOULD NOT FORSAKE THE ONE, NOT EVEN FOR THE NINETY-NINE; AND HE DID NOT FORSAKE ME.

We all can be leaky vessels. The living water can drain or gush from us, even when we've been rock solid for a long time. The mighty can fall, and crack, and break, and lose it. The God of the Bible can call forth a child from a 90-year-old womb, and He can piece you back together—or reforge you—stronger and larger and more capable than before, if . . . you humble yourself and put Him back on the throne of your life. The miraculous thing is that to put Him back requires only a single honest thought; even a small, but sincere desire for Him. The Bible says that if we have faith the size of a mustard seed, we can move mountains (Matt 17:20). The Holy Spirit will intercede when our words fail, and in a Holy Spirit flash—there is Jesus—not just holding out His hand, but holding you.

For though the righteous fall seven times, they rise again, but the wicked stumble when calamity strikes.
Proverbs 24:16

Passage 34:
Phone Tag with God

Have you ever played phone tag with someone? You leave a message to their message which was a message to your previous message? I once played what I felt like was "spiritual phone tag" with God. I knew I needed healing and I knew He'd restore me, but I wasn't quite ready to surrender it all to Him.

I acknowledged that I needed restoration. And as before, I knew He was there holding me; I didn't think He had stopped. But I couldn't yet fall completely in His loving lap and surrender all. He'd tell me what I needed to do and I'd say, "Yes, Lord. But not quite yet. Please give me till such and such a time and I will." Somedays, it would be more like, "Thank you—please just hold on a little while longer, and I'll do what I have to do, OK, Lord?" And He'd tell me what else to do, and back and forth we'd go.

I was feeling pressure and exhaustion from ministry work—what I call "working for God." I felt a sense of obligation to many people in my church. I had been a "success story;" came to Christ late in life, excelled at being a Sunday School teacher; went from saying "VBS -what?" to being a co-leader with Vacation Bible School. We endured the unsure times of 9/11 with a testimony from my husband that gave people goosebumps. Our sons were homeschooled and well-mannered. I didn't feel like I could say no to anything and I certainly couldn't not be what I felt people wanted me to be. And so, as the annual women's retreat for my church was approaching, that was when I chose to finally surrender. The emotions started the moment I pulled out of my driveway. I stopped the "spiritual phone tag" and rode the 170+ miles with Jesus.

I learned that He had more in store for me. He was putting me back together and I could see that I would not ever be the same again.

When you play phone tag with someone do you think of more things to say, or ask, than when you first called? Well, that might have been the case with me, but that wasn't with God. He knew His plan all along, and it was good. Now I know why He was so lovingly patient with me, and didn't knock me down before the retreat weekend!

There is a vast difference between just "working for God" and doing His work—the work He has designed and planned for you specifically, in advance (Eph 2:10). His plan for you is good. You just need to trust it. Be obedient to God, and to His will, and He will do a mighty work in you.

Because of your partnership in the gospel from the first day until now, being confident of this, that he who began a good work in you will carry it on to completion until the day of Christ Jesus.

Philippians 1:5-6

REWIND

Pain, patterns, and curses can be generational. I am blessed to say that those were broken with my life. All of my mother's siblings had failed marriages. Two aunts were remarried and then widowed. Each of my aunts and uncle had one child. And each of my cousins only had one child. I am the first in my family since my Gamma to have been in a long-term marriage (more than 34 years and counting), married only once, and to have had more than one child.

A good friend said to me after the death of her last parent, "I'm an orphan." I didn't understand then, but I do now. 2005 was the first year I didn't have a mom in the corporeal sense. As King David said when his son died, "he will not return to me but I will go to him" (2 Sam 12:23), I considered the same about Mom and me.

There was a day at the hospital when Momsie didn't want me in her room. She kept throwing me out and only allowed her sister in. I didn't know what I had done . . . I still don't. It may have been part of her illness or meds. What I saw was the bitterness of her life without Jesus. Just for a time. It had been disguised in the past as fearlessness, confidence, seriousness...but I instantly recognized it as the bitterness she had been wrestling with most of her life. It broke my heart. Mercifully, it didn't last. It accomplished what God wanted it to. I forgave her totally and in doing so discovered just how much I loved my mother.

Momsie would have loved the country setting of the Poconos. I wish she could have moved. I miss her. I wish she could return to me, but I will go to her.

Momsie and me, July 4, 1959

Passage 35:
WALKING IN DARKNESS

IT TOOK A YEAR. A YEAR OF DARK, DEEP, DEPRESSION TO GET ME BACK TO GOD, BACK TO JESUS, BACK TO THE HOLY SPIRIT. It felt like just when I would get over the hill, I would see the mountain. There was much I couldn't see though. Years ago, as I tried multilevel marketing, one of the phrases used in training said, "You don't know what you don't know." Until you know that you don't know, you are unteachable!

God began to show me how much I really didn't know. Didn't know of sin. Didn't know of surrender. Didn't know of obedience.

I went to the retreat to mourn; to "let it all go." What I found was that there was more to mourn in my life than I thought. I got a glimpse of how I had grieved God. I cried at the loss of the past, but I was beyond weeping when I caught a mere glimpse of the sorrow my past actions brought to God. Just as a mere reflection of God's glory turned Moses' hair white and was reflected in his skin, so can a mere glimpse of God's sorrow cause immense, internal, spiritual pain.

It was at the retreat that the speaker spoke of her own abortions and the toll that her actions wrought. Although I knew I had been forgiven, I recognized that I was carrying shame. That was not how God wanted me to live. He had lovingly brought me through those experiences so I could live a life that glorified Him and honored those lives.

I finally sought medical help from my Christian doctor and spiritual help from a Christian counselor. I'd love to say that those two actions brought me back, but the truth is that it was Jesus who used them and enabled me to see the light—His light!

When Jesus spoke again to the people, He said, "I am the light of the world. Whoever follows me will never walk in darkness, but will have the light of life."
John 8:12

Afterword

It's been a journey. Momsie left us over sixteen years ago, and I cannot count the number of times I have started to pick up the phone and call her. A historic ice storm, financial woes, graduations, my sons' first girlfriends, friends passing on, flat tires, new jobs, retirement parties, funny shows, broken hearts. Life.

There was no funeral. Mom wanted her body donated to science; not so altruistic, as economical, I believe. But I honored her wish. For a year, a local teaching hospital explored, and tested her earth suit, and I pray that she revealed secrets to them that have saved lives since. There was a memorial service held for the relatives and loved ones of all who did the same for the hospital in that year. I did not attend. I gave permission for her ashes to be scattered or disposed of however the institution chose. I held my own memorial service for her on February 25, 2005. It was a celebration of her life and attended by many.

I had said goodbye to Momsie days before the official date on her death certificate; assured in my own spirit that she was at peace, whole, and with our Lord. The celebration of life for a believer, and the funeral for the unbeliever are formalities for the living. It is a final chance to say goodbye; an opportunity to console those left, and the chance to share the hope of salvation with others. That's what happened at her memorial.

I have now been a child of God for more than twenty years. Although I had, in my humble opinion, moved past "kindergarten" faith-wise when Mom had been hospitalized, I certainly have matured more in the years since Mom left. But isn't that the point? If we "got" it all, why would God leave us here after our conversion? We are called to "work out our salvation" (Phil 2:12). What does that mean?

For me, it meant spending these last years on the rollercoaster of life. I'd be doing you a disservice to tell you that the Christian walk has been consistently easy or beautiful. It is the larger picture with all of the various pieces coming together that show a beautiful scene in the end. But some of those darker pieces, darker moments, are worth mentioning so that you can hear the conclusion of God's grace over my life.

Imagine a used, beat up cardboard box. It represents you, your life, your being, your sanity. Now load it up with a few "weights" of life. Sadness that has grown into depression. Annoyance that has turned into bitter anger. Loneliness. The day in and day out ... family, friends, kids, jobs, bills—life. Now further imagine that this cardboard box is becoming saturated with the metaphorical tears of frustration, and disappointment. Each "No" that you really needed to be a "Yes," all soaking through the cardboard box of your life. And you are trying to move around your world in such a state. Because of your faith, you know that the Holy Spirit is with you. But the burden gives the perception that the Holy Spirit is at best like duct tape on a wet cardboard box. Sticking here, coming loose there. You pray some more "Holy Ghost duct tape" on a spot, as another piece loses its grip.

That is how I had described my life at one point, even as a believer. My days started with me lying awake in bed but keeping my eyes shut. It was as if the day wouldn't start if I didn't look at my world. The first thoughts would be of disheartenment as I realized that I was no longer asleep and therefore I was not in a dream, but my reality. As I squinted to see what time it was, I was hoping that it was early enough that I could go back to sleep. Just dream a bit longer. Escape, avoid. I was so worn out and holding on with very, very saturated pieces of duct tape that were fast losing their stickiness.

Then came dark questions posing as potential solutions. "If I had a gun and put a garbage bag over my head, could I take a fatal shot and not have the bullet exit my skull and puncture the garbage bag so as to not leave a mess for my family to clean up?" "What if I waited until my husband's direct deposit cleared in the bank, packed up our sons and the van after he left for work, and drove as far and as long as possible before I had to stop?" Neither scenario seemed to be without glitches. So, I went through my day, and repeated the same questions as the days passed.

I felt like a wind-up toy that comes to a wall and just keeps bumping ... being pushed back a bit, but never advancing, waiting for the stored-up energy to be exhausted so it can stop. I lived like this for far too long. Lived? Existed.

The circumstances that had my mind in this awful spiral are truly not important. Different situations affect people in different ways. To be clear, I do not believe that all feelings of hopelessness have the same root cause. Some issues are emotional. Some are a response to incorrect thinking. Some are ideas that may have been fostered by outside forces—nurture and nature.

Some issues are the result of imbalances of a more "concrete" nature; hormonal and psychological imbalances that require much more than a course correction in thinking. Those causalities must be medically and professionally addressed. I possess neither skill set.

The truth is that God knows that this life is difficult. It is virtually impossible to live as we were designed to live because of sin and the architect of sin. God knows that we need Him. We must rely on Him and His power to succeed. We are too susceptible to the whispers of the serpent.

I struggled to carry my disintegrating, wet box of weights unnecessarily for too long. But I found my way out with a primary lesson that I could not grasp in fullness in any other relationship found here on earth, not even those redeemed for His glory, like that of me and Momsie.

God loves me. Now that seems like faith 101. I had to get that truth, that fact, from my head to my heart and into my very being. I had to accept it in my quietest, private moments where doubt would love to have its place. I had to accept it when others didn't reflect it. I had to accept it, even as my mind reflected on experiences that told me otherwise. I had to remove and actively replace every anchored lie that claimed it could never be dislodged.

Somewhere in my past the lie that claimed I was not deserving of love had lodged itself in my being. I had to divinely settle that. I had to learn that love is a verb, an action word. Only God's love is perfect—as God is love (1 John 4:8). In our imperfect state, when we love, even with our best intentions, it can still create struggle and pain. Yet, God's willingness to allow pain and struggle in our lives is the ultimate proof of His perfect love. Without the pain and struggle, we will not be ready for Him. Our faith, our character will not be strengthened. We will not recognize Him in all of His glory. We will not recognize how worthy He is of all of our praise.

I learned that this earthly life is so less important than I had imagined. As children of God, He longs for us to be home, in His presence for eternity. That is where our focus should be. We must understand that this is a temporary "green room," a waiting area for us to prepare ourselves for the glorious eternity that is to come. All of this corporeal life is so infinitesimally brief but we must understand its significance. This is a short race with a grand ending. At its end, we receive crowns of glory. That is why Paul encourages us with the reference to his own life as a race. I look forward to Heaven in a way that I cannot describe!

Once I totally embraced that I am loved by the Great I AM, the next step was to understand Who God is, and how His attributes relate to me, personally. I created a list that I refer to regularly. I've included it in the back of this book in the hopes that you will root yourself in the knowledge of your awesome Creator, as I have.

When I had a better grasp on who God really is, my box dried up and the weights got lighter. As I continue to "work out my salvation," my Holy Ghost tape is strengthened and I have peace and rest in God's truth.

At this stage of my life, having passed the age of 60, I can say with reasonable certainty, that there are fewer days ahead than behind. Medical advances notwithstanding, I doubt I'll see 120! My mother-in-law, who is 96 now, says "Time ain't as long as it has been!" When I say that to some people, they rebuke me a bit; as if I'm giving up or telling God to take me now. Far from it! I have found peace knowing some simple truths.

When I really examined my past, I saw the magnitude of my offense to God. While this sounds devastating, (and it was), it also came with benefits. The first benefit was a renewing of my gratitude for salvation. The second benefit was in that gratitude, a motivation to use these remaining years to honor God. He has allowed me to boldly, unashamedly, share my testimony in a way that exemplifies compassion to others who have traveled a similar road. In martial arts, the term sensei doesn't actually mean "teacher," but literally "one who has gone before." Taking that understanding, I realize that if I can accept the lessons learned from my loving Father, then I must pass on this wisdom to those who may be coming behind me in this life. To me, that is a call of love; of fellowship. I have learned to truly live without regret. There have been things in my humanity that I would have done differently. But all that has been filtered through His hands because He loves me and desires for me to become more like Christ Jesus.

My gracious sons fully took on the reflection of Christ's love and grace over me when I shared some of the dark moments of my past. As I held my breath in anticipation of their potentially horrified reaction, they looked at each other, and without missing a beat said, "So we have four siblings in heaven? We can't wait to meet them!" It was certainly a moment where I understood the scripture where Jesus references that we are to become "like" the little children; full of His grace, love, and innocence.

As a result of the pain of my past, I have now taken up the cause of the preborn who were rejected before birth, and the

My firstborn - Aren Michael

mothers who made that painful choice, as I had. As my mother had almost done. I am a visible testament to God's forgiveness and love. Like the woman with the alabaster jar in Luke 7, I love much because I have been forgiven much. I can extend that to others because I understand it so intimately.

I am eternity-minded. Not so much so as to be no earthly good, actually the opposite! I look at life differently and my quest is to see life, the world, and its events and people with the eyes and heart of Jesus. I know I won't get it right, but that's my quest. The Holy Grail. Until He returns or calls me home!

Now that Momsie is no longer here, I would gladly spend a year, a month, or a day with her. I was able to tell the darker side of the story because in the end we both found Christ as our Savior and we spent the last years as sisters-in-Christ; a miracle of the divine sovereignty of God. If you have a loved one from whom you are estranged, please don't give up hope! Jonah 2:8 says, "Those who cling to worthless idols forfeit the grace that could be theirs." The newer NIV translation says: "Those who cling to worthless idols turn away from God's love for them."

I never want to turn my back on God's grace, or His love. I pray the same for you.

Peace,
Saundra

The Essence of God and His Unmatched Love

- God is spiritual and at our essence, so are we. That will be how we commune with Him. I will shed my earth suit and live in a glorious body with Him in eternity. No pain, only joy.

- God is sovereign and is in absolute control. Everything is filtered through His hands. I trust Him.

- God is holy; pure, blameless, and flawless. Never will He make a mistake or do evil. In my anguish, I will not blame God but know that there will be victory.

- God is omnipresent. He has no bounds and can be with me always, everywhere.

- God is omnipotent. No one or thing has more power than Him. Creator of everything, He can defeat all of my enemies.

- God is immutable and will never change. He can never be any better or worse. He IS. I cannot change Him.

- God is truthful. He cannot lie to me and will always be accurate in His Word.

- God is wise and will never have a need for a plan B. His perfect will is enacted by the highest means and ends. Even when I cannot see it.

- God is good and desires to bless me and His creatures. He is no respecter of persons.

- God is gracious and freely gives salvation to all who call on Him. I am thankful that He heard my call.

- God is loving and has selfless love for His children, all of His children, equally. Even me.

- God is foreknowing. He is outside of time and knew each of us before we came to be. He knew my sins before I existed and still He loves me.

- God is righteous in wrath and therefore I desire to present myself pure and holy through the atoning sacrifice of Jesus Christ. Knowing that when I fail, I am forgiven.

And God is self-existent.
His aseity means that He has no need
or dependence on anyone.
Yet God chooses to be with us, with me.
With you.

I'd love for you to meet Momsie.

In the last REWIND I mentioned King David and what he said when his son died: 2 Samuel 12:23 - "he will not return to me but I will go to him."

The only way for you to meet Momsie is to be assured that you too will be in your heavenly home for all eternity. If you are not sure and you feel God's Holy Spirit calling to you, you can answer with a simple prayer such as the one below. The words aren't special, the surrender of your heart is.

Father God, I don't know everything about you, but I believe you love me. That you loved me enough to send your Son Jesus, as a baby, to live a sin free, human life and to satisfy your requirement of justice for my sins by His death on the cross. I thank you and I believe that He died for me. Today I recognize Your holiness and my sin and I repent. I ask for forgiveness of all of my sins and I accept the free gift of salvation that Jesus' death provides. I believe that Jesus rose again and when He did, He conquered sin and death for me. I now place You on the throne of my heart, believing that you will give me the Holy Spirit to teach and guide me until I am with You in Heaven. Amen.

See you in Heaven!

About the Author

After almost 40 years of what she refers to as her "wilderness wanderings," Saundra became a child of God on November 13, 1998. Her previous personal experiences, and new heart for the Lord aligned into the desire to help women fully embrace and accept the love God has for them, no matter their circumstance. In 2018, Saundra began Peer Counseling Training at the Pregnancy Resource Center of the Poconos in Pennsylvania where she completed the "Forgiven and Set Free" Bible study for post abortive women. She continues to volunteer weekly as a peer counselor and an after-abortion Bible study facilitator. In addition, Saundra recently completed the Psalm 51 Ministries Mentor Training. She is now a part of the nationwide Heart Helpers network of Christian sisters equipped to help other hurting women in their journey toward healing and wholeness found only in Christ.

Chayton, Kevin, and Aren
Mother's Day 2021

In an ironic twist, Saundra, a woman afraid of heights, realizes her most-dedicated ministry as a wife of nearly three-and-a-half decades to Kevin, a commercial pilot. Together, they have raised two handsome boys, Aren and Chayton. Blessed and redeemed by a life lit-up for the Lord, Saundra founded SonLit-Woods Ministries, where she brings together bold truth, love, and a touch of humor to speaking engagements and audiences around the world. Connect and laugh with Saundra at www.SonLitWoodsMinistries.com.

Additional copies of this book, now available at Amazon.com or BarnesandNoble.com.

www.ingramcontent.com/pod-product-compliance
Lightning Source LLC
La Vergne TN
LVHW090955080826
845145LV00003B/1013

9781736509401